# On The Policy Of The Soviet Union And The International Situation

# LEONID BREZHNEV

# On
# the policy
# of
# the Soviet Union
# and
# the international
# situation

Prepared by the Novosti Press Agency Publishing House, Moscow

DOUBLEDAY & COMPANY, INC.
GARDEN CITY, NEW YORK
1973

*Photographs courtesy of APN Publishing House, Moscow*

# CONTENTS

# GENERAL SECRETARY OF THE CENTRAL COMMITTEE OF THE COMMUNIST PARTY OF THE SOVIET UNION

## Leonid Ilyich Brezhnev

LEONID ILYICH BREZHNEV was born into a Russian worker's family on December 19, 1906, in the town of Dneprodzerzhinsk (called Kamenskoye at that time), a major steel center in the Ukraine. His father worked at the local steel mill his whole life, and subsequently Leonid Ilyich worked there as a worker and after graduating from a metallurgical institute, as an engineer. His younger brother and sister also worked at the same plant. As L. I. Brezhnev recalls, his family, truly a worker's dynasty, gave a total of almost a hundred years of labor to that steel mill.

The start of Leonid Brezhnev's working career coincided with the early years of the Soviet state, which was engendered by the Great October Socialist Revolution. The people, who set themselves the task of building a fundamentally new society, had first of all to revive the economy, devastated in the years of the First World War, the Civil War and foreign intervention. With their selfless efforts, the Soviet people transformed old, backward Russia into a new, socialist state. They built modern factories, power plants and schools and set up large-scale mechanized collective farms where for centuries small, primitive, and frequently semi-impoverished peasant households had eked out a bare existence. It was in this period that the generation to which L. I. Brezhnev belongs, shaped up in the Soviet Union.

Infected by the enthusiasm of that difficult, but heroic period, Leonid Brezhnev joined the Young Communist League at the age of 17. In 1929 he became a candidate member and in 1931 a member of the Communist Party. The purpose of his life now was to serve the cause of the emancipated people, of building communism.

Starting from 1927, after graduating from a specialized secondary school for land management and reclamation in Kursk, Central Russia, Leonid Ilyich worked as a surveyor in Kursk Guberniya and then in the Urals, dealing with matters of the system of land tenure for the toiling peasantry. This work in the midst of the people turned out to be excellent schooling, it enabled him to gain a deep insight into rural life and it revealed and developed his ability of an organizer. Shortly afterward the young surveyor was elected to the local government body, the District Soviet.

The country's new industry required new cadres of technical experts. Leonid Brezhnev enrolled at a metallurgical institute and after graduation, in 1935, returned to his birthplace to work as an engineer in the steel mill. Three years later he was elected to a leading party post, secretary of the Communist Party Regional Committee in Dnepropetrovsk, one of the biggest industrial areas of the country.

In June 1941 the Nazis attacked the Soviet Union and Brezhnev, like millions of men his age, went off to the battlefront. He remained in the field during the entire war. Serving with the 18th army, he took an active part in a number of military operations, including the heroic amphibious operation in the area of Novorossiisk (it has gone down in history by the name of Malaya Zemlya—minor land) on the Black sea coast.

Among the Soviet soldiers who fought for the liberation of Poland and Czechoslovakia and drove the fascists out of Hungary was Major General Brezhnev, a member of the Military Council and Chief of the Political Department of the Fourth Ukrainian Front.

After the war, as leader of the party organization of Zaporozhye Region and later Dnepropetrovsk Region in the Ukraine,

L. I. Brezhnev gave a great deal of his strength and energy to help restore the economy of these areas.

His practical experience in industry and agriculture and his political activity in the army brought out in full degree L. I. Brezhnev's talents as an outstanding organizer and party and government leader. As head of the Communist Party of Moldavia in 1950–1952, he supervised the job of developing the republic's industry and agriculture and raising its cultural standards.

In the mid-fifties the country began large-scale development of the virgin lands in the East. The goal was a major increase in Soviet agricultural output. Leonid Brezhnev was assigned to an executive post in the Communist Party of Kazakhstan, a republic where in that period, through the efforts of enthusiastic young people from all parts of the country, millions of acres of land were plowed for the first time and a major new grain-growing center developed.

In subsequent years, holding a top party post in Moscow, L. I. Brezhnev worked on the advancement of heavy industry and construction and the reinforcement of the country's defense capacity. A prime example of the accomplishments of Soviet industry, science and technology in that period was the world's first manned space flight, made by a Soviet man, Yuri Gagarin. This flight ushered in a new era in human history. L. I. Brezhnev, then Secretary of the Central Committee of the Communist Party of the Soviet Union, immediately became involved in organizing diverse projects linked with space exploration.

L. I. Brezhnev was elected to the Central Committee of the party at the Nineteenth CPSU Congress in 1952, and afterwards, became an alternate member of the Presidium and Secretary of the Central Committee of the CPSU. Starting from June 1957, he held the post of a member of the Presidium of the CPSU Central Committee, the party's highest body between plenary meetings of the Central Committee (since 1966 the Presidium is called the Politburo of the CC). At the same time, L. I. Brezhnev took a very active part in the work of the highest organs of state power. From 1960 to 1964 he was President of the Presidium of the USSR Supreme Soviet and in this capacity helped improve the functioning of the Soviets of Working People's Deputies and devoted much attention to the expansion of the Soviet Union's friendly ties with foreign states. After his election in 1964 to the party's highest post, he continued to take part in the work of the USSR Supreme Soviet as a member of its Presidium.

At the October plenary meeting of the CPSU Central Committee in 1964, L. I. Brezhnev was elected First Secretary (from 1966 onward, General Secretary) of the Central Committee of the Communist Party of the Soviet Union.

The work done by L. I. Brezhnev at his top party and government posts required tremendous, intensive effort. It embraces the widest range of problems, issues, cares and duties: from the elaboration, jointly with his colleagues, of basic principles and trends of policy to guidance in the solution of many practical problems concerning the development of the national economy, the strengthening of the defense capability, the advancement of science, technology and culture, and the raising of living standards of the working people—such is the range of this activity in the field of home policy. Leonid Brezhnev's name is inseparably linked, in particular, with the program for a large-scale increase in Soviet agricultural production, which he outlined in his reports at the plenary meetings of the CPSU Central Committee in March 1965 and May 1966.

This program, endorsed by the party congresses and highest government bodies, is now being successfully implemented.

In March 1966, in the main report of the Central Committee delivered by L. I. Brezhnev at the Twenty-third CPSU Congress, the principal tasks of the Eighth Five-Year Economic Development Plan of the USSR were defined, and many important questions of theory and practice of the building of communism were developed further.

A major event in the life of the party and the entire Soviet people was the Twenty-fourth CPSU Congress, held in March and April 1971. The experience accumulated by the party and the country in the preceding five-year period was analyzed, and major issues of the party's economic policy and the development of Soviet society at the modern stage were elaborated, in the main report of the Central Committee, delivered by L. I. Brezhnev.

In the sphere of economic policy the party line is designed to improve the living conditions of the Soviet people, L. I. Brezhnev pointed out at the congress. Without slighting the development of heavy industry, including its defense branches, the party sets forth as the main practical task of its economic program a considerable increase in the standard of living. This is our goal, he declared, and to attain it we must use to the full all the reserves, all the opportunities inherent in our economy. In the sphere of social policy the party line is designed to further strengthen the unity of Soviet society, to bring still closer together the classes and social groups, all the nations and nationalities that make up Soviet society. It aims to consistently develop socialist democracy, to enlist increasing numbers of people in the management of public and state affairs. It is a line for the all-out development of science and culture, and for further intellectual development of the Soviet people.

Extensive and diversified is the work of the General Secretary of the CPSU Central Committee and a member of the Presidium of the USSR Supreme Soviet in the field of international relations.

In foreign policy L. I. Brezhnev, expresses the consistent position of the Communist Party of the Soviet Union, adhering undeviatingly to the basic principles of the country's foreign policy worked out by the founder of the Soviet state, Vladimir Ilyich Lenin. These are the principles of peace and friendship, mutually beneficial cooperation among peoples, respect for the sovereign rights of bigger and smaller nations. This is a policy of the resolute rebuff of aggression, in other words, the policy known to the whole world as the policy of peaceful coexistence.

Taking this policy, L. I. Brezhnev has made a number of trips to Europe, Asia and Africa as head of peace-and-friendship missions and government and party delegations, and has had talks with many foreign leaders visiting the Soviet Union.

L. I. Brezhnev is deeply concerned with the consolidation and further development of cooperation among the socialist states, for their joint action in the interest of world peace and security of nations.

In his statements L. I. Brezhnev has formulated the most important principles and initiatives of Soviet foreign policy. A particularly concentrated expression of this is provided in the pertinent section of the report of the General Secretary of the CPSU Central Committee at the Twenty-fourth Party Congress, the section that has become known in many countries now as the Soviet Peace Program.

L. I. Brezhnev is particularly concerned with problems of strengthening peace and security and establishing good neighbor relations among the states.

L. I. Brezhnev's outstanding services during the war years and in his peacetime work have been honored with the country's highest decorations. He is a Hero of the Soviet Union and a Hero of Socialist Labor, and has been awarded four Orders of Lenin as well as other orders and medals.

L. I. Brezhnev has close ties with the people, often meets workers and collective farmers, servicemen and scientists. He enjoys well-deserved prestige and respect among the Soviet people. All who have happened to meet L. I. Brezhnev know him as a modest, easy-mannered, friendly and cordial person.

# Part I

LENIN'S CAUSE LIVES ON AND TRIUMPHS

# I

# V. I. LENIN—THINKER
# AND REVOLUTIONARY

Comrades, let us turn in our mind's eye to the nineteenth century. That was a time when capitalism ruled supreme. The rulers of the capitalist world garnered fabulous profits from exploitation of the masses, colonial plunder and wars of aggrandisement. The ideologists of the bourgeoisie vied with each other in prophesying the advent of the "golden age" of capitalism.

But beneath the surface of bourgeois prosperity powerful social forces were already burgeoning to overthrow the exploiting system. In 1848, Karl Marx and Frederick Engels, in their immortal *Manifesto of the Communist Party*, proved that the revolutionary substitution of socialism for capitalism was inevitable, and gave the working-class movement its fighting slogan—"Workers of all countries, unite!" In 1871, the first proletarian revolution flashed across the horizons of our planet: the Paris Commune raised aloft its red banner. The Communards suffered defeat, but the cause for which they had fought could not be defeated. The ranks of the proletariat multiplied, its organisation and consciousness were enhanced, and class hatred for the oppressors became more acute. Marxist ideas spread ever wider within the working-class movement.

At the turn of the century, capitalist society entered its last, imperialist stage of development. The epoch of revolutionary storms and social upheavals was at hand.

The prerequisites for revolution were coming to a head most swiftly in Russia. Oppression by the landowners and the bourgeoisie of Russia and of other countries, the deprived condition of dozens of oppressed nationalities, arbitrary rule by bureaucratic officials and police strong-arm methods, and the chronic abomination of the autocracy, as Lenin put it—all this caused growing indignation among the masses, and made Russia the ganglion of socio-political contradictions and conflicts of the coming epoch of imperialism. It was the proletariat of Russia that was destined to undertake the fulfilment of the most revolutionary of all the tasks of the international working-class movement of the time—to blaze mankind's path to socialism.

There was need for a man capable of continuing the cause of Marx and Engels, of obtaining a profound insight into the substance of the imminent revolutionary change, and of giving a lead to the social forces destined to carry out this change. This man was Vladimir Ilyich Ulyanov-Lenin.

What Lenin confronted as he was faced with a choice of a way in life was the tragedy of lone revolutionaries, who had stormed the autocracy from generation to generation, and had gone down in the unequal battle. But for Lenin that choice depended on the way that was to take the whole of Russia out of the dead end into which the protracted domination of darkest reaction had led her. Lenin found the answer to this question in the works of Marx.

On the basis of Marxist theory, Lenin demonstrated that Russia was developing according to the same laws as any other capitalist country. Lenin gave the scientific backing for this conclusion in a number of fundamental studies, including such of his works as *What the "Friends of the People" Are and How They Fight the Social-Democrats* and *The Development of Capitalism in Russia*.

Indeed, Russia was moving along the capitalist way, and the working class was becoming the chief revolutionary force.

That is why Lenin fought the Narodniks, who were proponents of an "original," i.e., petty-bourgeois, socialism. But even as he dealt his blows against Narodism Lenin was aware of another danger: the attempts to use Marxism to embellish capitalism in Russia. This meant another battle, this time against the "legal Marxists," who sought to turn Marx into a common liberal, and against the "economists," who sought to make the young working-class movement politically blind.

That was the start of the formation of Leninism in the struggle to safeguard the revolutionary teachings of Marx and Engels. That was the beginning of the preparation of revolution in Russia, an endeavour to which Lenin gave 30 years of his life.

Lenin undeviatingly responded to Marx's call not only to *explain* but also to *change* the world. Solving theoretical problems in close connection with practice, with the class struggle, was a quality of Lenin's genius which met the fundamental need of the revolutionary movement in the 20th century, when the proletarian revolution came on the order of the day.

Revolutionary thinking on a high plane and unsurpassed skill in organising the class struggle of the proletariat were both part of Lenin's make-up. As no other man he was aware that victory of the revolution and construction of a new society demanded a militant working-class party equipped with the theory of Marxism. In his well-known work, *What Is to Be Done?*, he wrote: "Give us an organisation of revolutionaries, and we will overturn Russia!"

He made it his life's work to create and temper such a party, the Bolshevik Party. What was required was a party capable of leading the masses and taking them into battle against tsarism, a party prepared not only to win Russia from the landowners and the bourgeoisie, but also to rule Russia, and ensure the triumph of the proletarian dictatorship. It was to establish such a party that Lenin waged a relentless struggle against the Mensheviks, the Trotskyites and opportunists of every stripe. The new type of party is, comrades, the supreme embodiment of the indissoluble unity of revolutionary theory and revolutionary practice. It is the greatest legacy that Lenin has bequeathed to the world revolutionary movement, to the builders of socialism and communism.

When Lenin started on his activity as revolutionary, there were only a few dozen Marxists in Russia. When Lenin's party came to power, it had 350,000 men in its ranks followed by millions. It was a victory for Lenin and the Leninists, a victory which enabled Russia—and the whole world with her—to take a step into a new historical epoch.

The battles of three Russian revolutions produced and put to the test new theoretical conclusions and generalisations, and new strategic and tactical propositions which made up the basis of Lenin's theory of socialist revolution.

The 1905–1907 revolution was the first test. The works which Lenin wrote in that period constitute eight great volumes. Among them are such fundamental works as *Two Tactics of Social Democracy in the Democratic Revolution* and *The Agrarian Programme of Social Democracy in the First Russian Revolution, 1905–1907,* his speeches at the Third, Fourth and Fifth Congresses of the RSDLP, together with hundreds of articles ranging over every aspect of the revolutionary struggle, without exception.

Summing up the experience of the masses in struggle, to counter the dogmatic schemes of the Mensheviks, Lenin pointed to the real possibility, in the conditions of imperialism, of the bourgeois-democratic revolution growing into a socialist revolution. Lenin's teaching on the hegemony of the proletariat in the bourgeois-democratic revolution, on the revolutionary-democratic dictatorship of the proletariat and the peasantry, on the attitude to other classes and parties, and on the tactics of the proletarian party in periods of revolutionary upswing and downswing—all of this even today constitutes the Bolshevik "model tactics for all" who have still to overthrow the exploiting system.

Lenin's theoretical thinking is so penetrating and profound and carries such general significance for the world revolutionary movement because his ideas were shaped on the sound basis of dialectical and historical materialism, and have themselves always contributed to the creative development of the latter. Lenin regarded the party, class approach to social phenomena as an organic principle of Marxist ideology. He taught Communists to look beyond every political trend, programme and declaration, beyond every social and moral doctrine to the interests of definite classes, and to determine their attitude to them from the proletarian standpoint.

Lenin held the connection of theory and practice, philosophy and politics to be a law governing the activity of the whole party. That is why after the defeat in the 1905 revolution, when the sway of reaction in the country, and the confusion and vacillation in the Party posed a threat to the theoretical foundation of the proletarian movement, Lenin turned the whole power of his genius to the defence and further development of the philosophical legacy of Marx and Engels.

Lenin saw the scientific discoveries of his day as the start of a deep-going revolution in natural science, which has assumed such a tempestuous pace in our day. The ideas and conclusions formulated in his book, *Materialism and Empirio-Criticism*, have been brilliantly confirmed by the subsequent development of science. To his dying day Lenin gave unflagging attention to providing the theoretical grounds for the Party's activity, ceaselessly enriching and developing Marxist philosophy.

With splendid mastery of the whole arsenal of Marxist theory, a brilliant strategist and tactician, a man totally free of the slightest semblance of dogmatism, Lenin was prepared to meet any turn in historical events. He clearly saw that the imperialist world war had started a general crisis of the capitalist system latent with a revolutionary explosion of tremendous force. From then on Lenin devoted the whole of his activity to show that the revolution was near, and to prepare it.

From the beginning of the war, the Bolsheviks, led by Lenin, issued a challenge to the forces of chauvinism and opportunism. Just think, comrades, of the strength of purpose, of the courage, the faith in the justice of one's cause, in the certain victory of the revolutionary cause that were required to proclaim, in the atmosphere of supreme chauvinist intoxication, a slogan urging the defeat of "one's own" government, and to issue a call to transform the imperialist war into a civil war! That is what Lenin and the Bolsheviks did. They declared an implacable struggle against the leaders of the Second International, who had betrayed the working-class cause. They began to rally the healthy, internationalist forces in the world working-class movement, the forces which were destined to become the basis of the new, communist International.

It is to the period of the imperialist war more than to any other period of Lenin's life that these words of his best apply:

"There it is, my fate. One fighting campaign after another—against political stupidities, philistinism, opportunism and so forth.

"It has been going on since 1893. And so has the hatred of the philistines on account of it. But still, I would not exchange this fate for 'peace' with the philistines."

An impassioned fighter of the revolution, Lenin was also its most profound thinker. During the war, he carried on a vast amount of scientific work in analysing the essence of monopoly capitalism, which had started the world-wide slaughter. The result of Lenin's economic research over many years was the creation of a coherent theory of imperialism as the highest and final stage of capitalism. Marx's economic teaching was raised to a new stage.

The theorists of opportunism probed the new phemonena of the imperialist epoch to find justification for their assertions that capitalism had become "organised," and "regulated," and justification for abandoning the revolution. Lenin started a relentless struggle against these apologists of imperialism. He proved that it was precisely the new features of capitalism that opened up fresh possibilities and fresh prospects for the proletariat's victorious struggle against the bourgeoisie, and demanded an intensification of this struggle; he proved that imperialism is the eve of the socialist revolution. One of the discoveries of Lenin's genius in this context is the conclusion that the socialist revolution can win initially in a few countries or even in one country.

All this has become a part of the treasure house of Leninism, and is being used as a victorious weapon by our Party and other Marxist-Leninist parties.

The February Revolution of 1917 confronted the Bolshevik Party and the proletariat of Russia with a host of totally new problems. Today it is clear to everyone that the bourgeois-democratic revolution was bound to grow into a socialist revolution. However, we should bear in mind the highly confused and contradictory situation at that time, and the great diversity of views then concerning the further way the revolution was to take, in order to appreciate afresh Lenin's wisdom, perspicacity and strength of purpose, and to sense the real proportions of his achievement. His *April Theses*, which marked out a clear prospect for transition to the socialist revolution, was not only an event which marked a fundamental turning point in the political history of our country but also another step forward in the development of the Marxist theory of revolution as a whole.

Upon his return to Russia, Lenin threw himself into the practical effort of preparing the socialist revolution. He was the acknowledged proletarian leader, and the focus of all the multifarious Party activity, which abounded in unforeseen events and dangers. In his works the principles of strategy and tactics which he formulated, and which helped the Bolshevik Party to display such unsurpassed skill in leading the masses from February to October, are elaborated into generalisations on a much broader plane. Lenin made it clear that in Russia the economic and political prerequisites for socialist revolution had matured, and prepared the Party for the most diverse forms of political and armed struggle to overthrow capitalism. In such of his works as *Marxism and Insurrection*, and *Advice of an Onlooker*, among others, he sets out a coherent theory of armed uprising as an art.

At the same time Lenin saw in the development of the revolution in Russia and pointed it out to the Party, an extremely rare possibility offered by history, which, he said, was extremely valuable, the possibility of the peaceful transition of power into the hands of the working class. Events took a turn that sent the Russian revolution along a different, non-peaceful way. But the very fact that he posed the question of a possibility, in principle, of the revolution developing along one of two ways is in itself an achievement of Lenin's thinking which is meaningful to this very day.

On the very eve of the October Revolution, during his last period underground, Lenin concentrated on working out such problems crucial for the victory of socialism as the dictatorship of the proletariat, socialist democracy, and the two phases of communist society. That was the origin of *The State and Revolution,* one of Lenin's outstanding works.

Relying on the creative initiative of the revolutionary masses, Lenin worked out the theory of the Soviet state as a form of the proletarian dictatorship. The basic principles of Soviet power, which Lenin worked out, retain their significance for every working people's state supplanting the bourgeois state. This has now been proved by the experience of socialist revolutions in other countries.

The victory of the Great October Socialist Revolution, won under the leadership of the Bolshevik Party headed by Lenin, was an event of world historical importance. It marked the start of the revolutionary transformation of the world. At the same time, it was the culminating point of the whole of Lenin's preceding theoretical and practical activity. Some days, and even hours, in the lives of men are equivalent to decades. Such was the period of the October Revolution for Lenin. All his knowledge, all his vast political experience, all his will-power and energy were concentrated on preparing the uprising.

In that period, Lenin repeatedly recalled the famous slogan of the revolutionaries of the past: "Boldness, boldness and yet more boldness!" A consistent opponent of any adventurism, a flexible and circumspect politician, Lenin was a model of revolutionary boldness, resoluteness, and purposefulness, and taught the Party to act likewise. When it became clear that the situation had matured and that the uprising was inevitable and necessary—everything had to be thrown onto the scales of history. The Party did so at the call of Lenin and the Central Committee, which he led—and won. The Great October Revolution is a real triumph of the Leninist strategy and tactics of the class struggle, of the Leninist theory of revolution.

The Winter Palace was taken by storm. The last bourgeois government of Russia had fallen. Vladimir Ilyich Lenin became the head of the world's first workers' and peasants' government. A tireless fighter for the triumph of socialist ideas, Lenin became the architect and the builder of the majestic edifice of socialism.

Lenin directed the defence of the Soviet Republic, and the formation of the Red Army. He found the solution of the most complex questions of development of the socialist economy and laid the foundations of the political economy of socialism. His ideas became the basis of the first Constitution of the RSFSR and of the formation of the Union of Soviet Socialist Republics. He had in his field of vision every sphere—culture and education, science and technology, the destiny of classes and the destiny of nations. In a little over six years after the victory of October, the leader of our revolution performed a gigantic amount of work, whose content and results will long continue to exert an influence on the course of world history.

But whatever the questions Lenin dealt with, whatever the problems he tackled, his attention was always focused on the Party, on the tempering and strengthening of its ranks. He regarded factionalism and group action in the Party as the greatest evil, which had to be fought resolutely and relentlessly. Lenin's brilliant speeches at the Party Congresses after the October Revolution, permeated with the breath of the revolution, to this day continue to be models of the principled political analysis, and the implacable attitude to ideological and political vacillation. The unity of the Party, for which

Lenin worked with such fervour, was, is and will continue to be one of the most important sources of all our victories.

Lenin gave much energy to developing the world communist movement, to preparing the political army of the world socialist revolution. The Communist International was set up on his initiative. This marked a turning point in the history of world communism. Lenin has left us an integrated concept of the world revolutionary process in the new epoch of which the pivot is the struggle between the two social systems. He developed the Marxist propositions on proletarian socialist internationalism. Lenin's speeches at the Congresses of the Comintern, and his classical work, *"Left-Wing" Communism—An Infantile Disorder*, to this day continue to be an encyclopaedia of the strategy and tactics of the world communist movement.

Marxism-Leninism is a coherent international teaching, it is a theory which belongs to all Communists and all revolutionaries, and serves them as a guide to action.

Historical experience has left nothing of the attempts by bourgeois and revisionist ideologists to set Lenin against Marx, to contrast Leninism and Marxism, depicting Leninism as a specifically Russian, national phenomenon. Indeed, Lenin had been born in Russia and had fought for a socialist Russia. But he had never regarded the revolution in Russia otherwise than as a component part and factor of the world revolution. Lenin's teaching incorporated everything that had been produced by mankind's best minds, generalising and fusing into a single whole the world-wide experience of the working people's class struggle.

Lenin watched with great attention the development of the economic and political struggle of the working class of Europe and America, painstakingly comparing and evaluating the various forms of this struggle. He took a keen interest in the problems of the national-liberation movement. He made a deep study of the various aspects of the life and struggle of all working people, drawing on the practice of the class struggle in the various countries for lessons to apply to the revolutionary theory and tactics of the world liberation movement.

It was natural, therefore, that representatives of the revolutionary workers of the whole world should turn to Lenin, the great theorist and leader possessing a vast wealth of knowledge and experience.

In our own day, all those who are fighting for the victory of socialism and communism turn to Lenin and his teaching. "Leninism is the Marxism of the epoch of imperialism and proletarian revolutions," as the Centenary Theses of the CPSU Central Committee say, "the epoch of the collapse of colonialism and the victory of national-liberation movements, the epoch of mankind's transition from capitalism to socialism and the building of communist society."

Leninism is the most advanced and influential ideology of the modern world, the invincible ideology of those who have the future with them. The works of no other man have been so widely read as are those of V. I. Lenin. They have been published in 117 languages of the world. Lenin's books have been printed in hundreds of millions of copies. They are being read by men in all countries and on all continents, helping them to live and struggle.

Explaining the reasons for the successes of scientific communism, Lenin wrote: Marxist teaching is all-powerful because it is true. These words fully apply to the teaching of Lenin himself. The truth of Lenin's teaching has been confirmed by life itself, by the whole experience of political development in the 20th century.

Progressive mankind pays the tribute of profound respect to Lenin, the brilliant theorist and the great architect of socialism. At the same time, Vladimir Ilyich Lenin is a man whom we all cherish and whom many generations after ours will continue to cherish for his supreme qualities as fighter and revolutionary, a man of spotless purity, and of exceptional personal charm.

Lenin had great affection for men, he fought for their happiness, and for the sake of this took an implacable attitude to oppressors and exploiters, to their hired servitors, whatever their make-up, to renegades and traitors to the revolutionary cause.

A principled approach, straightforwardness and truthfulness in everything were the distinctive features of Lenin's style of work. He was an irreconcilable opponent of loud talk, "revolutionary idle chatter," and communistic self-conceit. Whatever the situation, whatever the circumstances, Lenin retained his clear and realistic approach to facts and events, an ability to discover and expose any mistakes in good time, and determination to secure their correction.

Maxim Gorky wrote that "one half of Lenin's great soul lived in the future." That is, indeed, very true. Lenin had the rare gift of seeing in the present the future destiny of mankind. Never out of touch with life, with practice, with the real conditions and possibilities of the given historical period, Lenin projected his thought far ahead, into the future. He shed the light of scientific foresight to illumine the way lying ahead of the working class for many decades.

Lenin resolutely fought against any playing down of revolutionary theory, any emasculation of its creative character, or its reduction to a set of ready-made recipes. The whole of Lenin's life was ceaseless creative effort, creative effort in theory, in politics, in organising the class struggle, and in building up the Party and the state. This quality of always taking the creative approach he also fostered in the great Party which continues honourably to carry Lenin's banner, the banner of communism.

Lenin was unequalled in his ability to create an atmosphere of real collectivity in any work. While maintaining his standpoint with fervour, conviction and insistence, he valued the opinion of his comrades and was sensitive to what they said. He educated and united around himself a whole host of outstanding revolutionaries, political leaders and statesmen who came from the ranks of the people. Under Lenin's guidance, the Party's Congresses and the sittings of the Central Committee, its Politburo and the Council of People's Commissars were models of collective elaboration of policy, expressive of the interests of the working class and of all working people.

It sometimes seems inconceivable, surpassing the bounds of human possibility, that one man, even a genius, was able to perform the titanic work done by Lenin. He was a great and tireless worker, a man with a staggering capacity for work. To become a Communist, Lenin said, one has to assimilate the knowledge accumulated by mankind. That is the rule Lenin followed all his life. Wherever he was, be it the village of Shushenskoye in Siberia or the British Museum, a tsarist prison cell, Munich or Poronino, the libraries of Paris or Geneva, he continued to study works in philosophy and natural science, economics and sociology, history, military questions and international relations. All this wealth of human knowledge Lenin turned to the benefit of the revolutionary cause. Dozens of books and pamphlets, thousands of articles, reports and speeches, letters and notes—such is Lenin's boundless literary legacy which contains his political and revolutionary experience, his thoughts and observations.

Lenin lived for men and in their midst. He was closely connected with the revolutionary working-class movement in Petrograd, Moscow, and other proletarian centres of Russia. Wherever destiny took Lenin, wherever he found himself, and whatever he did, he was in touch with the people through a thousand links. Lenin felt an organic need to meet and talk with workers and peasants, soldiers, scientists and workers in culture. This was the politician's need to compare his own conclusions with the experience of the masses, to test the broad generalisations against what appeared to be the particular cases and the personal destinies of those who carried out the revolution and built socialism. At the end of December 1921, while sketching out the draft theses on the role and tasks of the trade unions, Lenin wrote: the thing is to live in the midst of the masses, to know their moods, to know everything, to understand them, and to know how to approach them. These words best reflect Lenin's style, which has become a model for the Party he founded, for the Communists of the whole world.

Modesty and simplicity, genuine humanity, respect for and trust in men, and a personal concern for their destiny were combined in Lenin with a principled firmness, and exactingness towards himself and others; wisdom and foresight with a tireless, persevering efficiency and indomitable will; the erudition and keen mind of the great scientist with a sincere love of life, of its true values and joys.

Such was Vladimir Ilyich Lenin, thinker, revolutionary, man. His teaching will always be a call and a guide to action, and his life's work an inspiring example for Communists and for millions of other men.

# II

# LENINISM—
# BANNER OF COMMUNIST
# CONSTRUCTION

Comrades, the proletarian anthem, *The Internationale,* contains these remarkable words: "No more tradition's chains shall bind us, arise, ye slaves, no more in thrall! The earth shall rise on new foundations, we have been naught, we shall be all." The working class of our country became the first contingent of the international army of labour to raze the old, capitalist world, and to create a new, socialist world.

## 1. Victory of Socialism in the Soviet Union—a Triumph of Leninism

Lenin held the creative activity of the victorious proletariat to be its main task. But to make a start on construction there was a need to beat back the joint attack of the armed foreign intervention and internal counter-revolution. The workers and peasants of Soviet Russia rallied round Lenin's Party, while relying on the powerful international support of the working people of other countries, and succeeded in winning their victory. Imperialism suffered a major military-political and moral defeat.

The young Soviet state born of the revolution—the state of the proletarian dictatorship—withstood the onslaught. Millions of men, inspired by Lenin's idea of restructuring society on socialist lines, started to build the new life.

Lenin warned that the road to socialism "will never be straight; it will be incredibly involved." But even in the most difficult conditions, Lenin did not lose faith in the titanic possibilities of the working people, the revolutionary working class and the Communist Party.

It called for all-penetrating depth of thought, breadth of outlook and boldness of idea to preserve clarity of orientation in a Russia disrupted and ploughed up by war and revolution, in the labyrinthine entanglement of socio-economic tendencies, political forces, and contradictory views and moods, and to find and present in a theoretically faultless form the main, principal lines of advance towards socialism. And that is just what Lenin did.

The New Economic Policy, industrialisation, collectivisation, the cultural revolution . . . These are all household words behind which lie a whole period in the history of our country, the destiny of classes and the biographies of men. These concepts are now in the textbooks. They have become the ABC of scientific communism. Lenin's profound ideas about the ways of creating a new society still serve as a reliable guide for the builders of the new world.

Lenin's plan for socialist construction is a model of the scientific, complex and realistic approach to the solution of a task of world historic importance. This plan ranged over all the tiers of the social edifice—the development of the productive forces, the transformation of social relations, and the recasting of man's spiritual world. Needless to say, it was based on the vast creative potential of the Party, the millions of builders of socialism, on the fact that in practice, in vibrant activity fresh possibilities were bound to open up, and new methods and means found for advancing towards the set goals. Lenin believed that the insuperable strength of the new social system lay in the unity of Marxist science, which determines the Party's programme propositions, and the initiative and historical creative endeavour of the masses.

Not everyone understood and accepted Lenin's idea that it was possible to build socialism in an economically backward, predominantly peasant country in a capitalist encirclement. The Right and the "Left" oppositionists strove to impose either capitulationist or adventurist ideas, and to get the country off the Leninist path. The political struggle, which became especially acute after Lenin's death, was protracted and intense. But Lenin's ideas triumphed.

The cause of socialist construction generated such a tide of revolutionary enthusiasm and inspired, dedicated labour that it literally swept away all the obstacles on the road to socialism. What was once a plan became reality. That was a world historic victory of the Soviet people, a triumph of Leninism.

In the 1930s, socialism was firmly established in every sphere of life in our country. The world saw a socialist industrial and collective farm power moving forward in a determined, powerful drive. Conditions were being created for the next great stride along the way mapped out by Lenin.

This was prevented by the war. The country was subjected to a piratical attack by the fascist invaders. A mortal danger confronted our country. It was then that the Soviet people's courage, steadfastness and indomitable will to victory, and their cohesion round the Leninist Party were displayed with unprecedented force. In the course of the stern ordeal, the Soviet social and state system demonstrated its unbreakable strength. Those harsh years reaffirmed the profound truth of Lenin's words when he said that a people defending its own power, and standing up for its just cause and its future can never be vanquished. At the cost of millions of lives of its sons and daughters the Soviet people safeguarded the gains of socialism.

We shall soon be marking the 25th anniversary of the victory over fascist Germany. On the eve of this notable date we pay fresh tribute to the great feat of the Soviet people and its Armed Forces. From generation to generation—forever—our people will honour the memory of those who gave their lives for the freedom and happiness of the Soviet people, for the sake of their native land.

Guided by Lenin's precepts we shall continue to strengthen our country's defences, and equip our Army with the most up-to-date weapons. Our Army was, is and will continue to be an army of peace, and a reliable bulwark of the security of all peoples.

Everyone is aware of the heavy losses and destruction which the war brought us. Many towns and villages, factories and power stations, schools and hospitals had to be built anew. Thwarting the enemies' treacherous plans to weaken our state for a long time, and healing the wounds of war in the shortest possible time, the Soviet people took a great stride forward. The material and spiritual gains achieved in the post-war years are staggering. Socialism has once again demonstrated its strength and viability.

Our Party and the Soviet people have accumulated a vast store of experience in the class struggle and social transformation. The innovatory character of these transformations demanded of the Party political and theoretical maturity, efficient organisation and steadfastness, consistency, and a thorough verification of the ways and means of building the new society. And, to use Lenin's words, this "experience . . . cannot be taken away, no matter how difficult the vicissitudes the Russian revolution and the international socialist revolution may pass through. It has gone down in history as socialism's gain, and on it the future world revolution will erect its socialist edifice."

The novelty, singularity, and the unprecedented scale of social change and economic construction, the lack of experience, and the frenzied resistance of the bourgeoisie—all made the struggle for socialism especially difficult, but immeasurably noble and heroic. "Let . . . the bourgeoisie . . . heap imprecations, abuse and derision upon our heads for our reverses and mistakes in the work of building up *our* Soviet system," wrote Lenin. "We do not forget for a moment that we have committed and are committing numerous mistakes and are suffering numerous reverses. How can reverses and mistakes be avoided in a matter so new in the history of the world as the building of an unprecedented *type* of state edifice! We shall work steadfastly to set our reverses and mistakes right and to improve our practical application of Soviet principles, which is still very, very far from being perfect. But we have a right to be and are proud that to us has fallen the good fortune to *begin* the building of a Soviet state, and thereby to *usher in* a new era in world history . . ."

As we look back on the road we have covered, we can say: indeed, our people and our Party have many things to take pride in. Many difficulties and adversities have fallen to the lot of the Soviet people. On their shoulders they have borne a tremendous historical responsibility. But courageously and steadfastly they have overcome all the trials, fulfilling their noble mission with dignity. Everywhere and always, in times of stern trial and fierce battle, in times of joyous victories and grievous setbacks, our people have remained loyal to the Leninist banner, loyal to their Party and to the cause of the revolution. On this momentous day, comrades, we can say that we have some achievements to report in honouring Lenin's memory. For the first time in the history of world civilisation, socialism has scored a full and final victory, a developed socialist society has been built and the conditions have been created for the successful construction of communism.

Soviet society today is powerful socialist industry and developed agriculture. Comparison is the best way to realise the scale of the modern economy. In five days our industry turns out more goods than the whole of industry in tsarist Russia produced in a year. The Soviet Union's national wealth has grown to great proportions—it is 15 times as much as before the revolution. Its value can no longer be expressed in ten figures: it now amounts to more than a million million roubles. Behind these figures lie the heroic labour of Soviet people, the construction of thousands of enterprises, and the development of new natural resources and economic areas.

Soviet society today is friendship and co-operation between all classes and social groups, all nations and nationalities, all generations; it is socialist democracy, which actually assures the working people of a part in the administration of all the affairs of state and society; it is advanced socialist science and culture, which belong to the mass of the people.

Soviet society today is the real embodiment of the ideas of proletarian, socialist humanism. It has placed the production of material values and the achievements of spiritual culture, the whole system of social relations, at the service of the man of labour. The Soviet people have already come to accept as a fact that the growth of production and the development of culture in our country lead to better conditions of life for the working people, for the whole people. This appears to be quite natural, it is not given too much thought, it is sometimes even forgotten. But, after all, it is, essentially, one of the basic distinctions between our system and capitalism, under which production is expanded to enrich the property owner and not to improve the life of the working man.

One of the greatest achievements of socialism is that every Soviet man is assured of his future. He is aware that his work, his abilities and his energy will always find a fitting use and appreciation. He is sure that his children will be given a free education and the opportunity of developing their talents. He knows that society will never abandon him in misfortune, that in the event of illness he will be given free medical treatment, a pension in the event of permanent disability, and security in old age.

Everything we have, everything we live by and take pride in is the result of the struggle and working endeavour of our working class, peasantry and intelligentsia, of the whole Soviet people.

The entire history of our society bears out the great truth of the Marxist-Leninist teaching about the working class being the leading revolutionary and creative force. The Soviet working class has brilliantly demonstrated its capacity to direct society, and build socialism and communism. It is the working class, above all, that has laboured to create all the country's industrial and defence might, the technical basis for the transformation of agriculture and the other branches of the economy. It has produced from its ranks thousands of statesmen and public leaders, commanders of production, scientists and military leaders, writers and artists. The working class, the most numerous and the best organised class, continues to play the leading role in our society.

Its goal—communism—has become the goal of the whole people.

Its ideology—Marxism-Leninism—has become the dominant ideology.

Its Party—the Communist Party—has become the party of the whole people.

The collective-farm peasantry is a reliable ally of the working class in struggle and in labour. Socialism has put an end once and for all to the poverty, deprivation and ignorance of the peasants, and has helped them to escape from the narrow world of individualism. Collective labour on socialised land has transformed the everyday life and spiritual atmosphere in the countryside. More than three million farm-machine operators, hundreds of thousands of agronomists, livestock experts, engineers, teachers and doctors work in the villages. Our collective-farm peasantry is a new socialist class, and an active builder of communist society.

At every stage of the socialist revolution, in the course of socialist construction, and today, when the Soviet people are building communism, the alliance of the working class and the peasantry has always constituted the solid foundation of our system, and the pledge of fresh victories on the way to communism!

Lenin's prediction of a future alliance of the working class and the representatives of science and technology, which "no dark force can withstand," as Lenin put it, has come true. To-day, we pay a great tribute of respect and gratitude to Soviet scientists, whose role is especially great in this age of the most profound social, scientific and technical change. In the ranks of our fine Soviet intelligentsia are millions of engineers, technicians, teachers, workers in public health, workers in the arts, and functionaries of the administrative apparatus. The great intellectual potential, which our country has built up, is a major source of the progress of Soviet society.

Men of different generations march shoulder to shoulder in the ranks of the builders of communism under a common Leninist banner. Among them are those who laid the first stones in the foundation of the socialist edifice, those who arms in hand fearlessly defended the gains of socialism, those who rebuilt our towns and villages from the ruins and ashes, and those who are still young, and are just setting foot on life's highway.

The older generation of the fighters for socialism has brought up a generation fit to take over, passing on to the latter its experience and knowledge, handing on its victorious Leninist baton. The Party is quite sure that Soviet youth and its vanguard, the Leninist Komsomol, in whose ranks more than 100 million Soviet people have already had a political schooling, will bring glory to their country by fresh remarkable achievements.

The Soviet people have traversed a great and glorious road. Lenin's revolutionary words first rang out on our soil. His revolutionary cause was started and is being continued with success on our soil. Lenin's ideals permeate all our achievements and plans. By building the socialist society, the Soviet people have erected a majestic monument to their teacher and leader.

## 2. Leninism and Questions of Communist Construction

Comrades, all our Party, all the Soviet people live for a single cause. It is the cause of building a communist society. The ways leading to this great goal are defined in the Programme of the CPSU, and in the decisions of Party Congresses and CC Plenums, which have met with the approval of the whole people. The greater the tasks the Soviet people set themselves, the more responsible the Party's work becomes, and the greater the need to look to Lenin for advice. Lenin's ideas, his great practical experience as fighter and creator, are of invaluable assistance to us in solving the most important problems in the Soviet country's present-day development.

Since Lenin's death, life has gone a long way forward, much has changed, producing a great number of new phenomena and problems which it was hard even to imagine in his lifetime. But today, too, the key to their understanding and solution is provided by the laws of socialist development discovered by Lenin. That is why Lenin continues to be a living participant in our endeavour, and our sage and reliable teacher.

Just as every building is started from its foundations, so the creation of the material and technical basis occupies first place in the gigantic and many-faceted effort of communist construction.

The more than half a century of experience in socialist economic endeavour provides convincing confirmation that the direction of the economy is perhaps the most challenging and the most creative task of all those which arise after a revolution. Here, as in other spheres of social life, let us add, there are virtually no cut-and-dried solutions which one could adopt and get rid of all cares. The economy is a complex and dynamic organism whose development in itself continuously produces new problems.

The justice of this truth is especially evident today, when the Soviet economy is entering a new important stage. Our socialist production has grown to vast proportions, the interconnections in our national economy have become more complex, and the scientific and technical revolution is advancing at a headlong pace. In view of all this the Party's Central Committee and the Government have arrived at the conclusion that it is necessary to work out an economic policy, methods of conducting economic operations, and forms of organisation and administration that will meet the present stage of the country's development. As we look back we feel justified in saying that the 23rd Congress of the CPSU and the Central Committee Plenary Meetings, from those of March and September of 1965 to the December Plenary Meeting of last year, have enabled us to make a serious advance in this direction.

The 24th Congress of the Party is now at hand. Preparation of the plan for the next five years is nearing completion. In other words, we are to take new major decisions to determine the ways for developing the Soviet economy over a considerable period ahead.

We aim at a Leninist approach to this great undertaking, bringing out from the whole diversity, the whole range of economic tasks the main and principal link. It is to enhance the effectiveness of social production, and bring about a considerable increase in labour productivity in every sphere. Lenin pointed to the decisive importance of this aspect of our endeavour in the early years of the Soviet power. With our present level of socialist economic development, we have real possibilities of ensuring rapid economic growth, primarily by intensifying development in every branch.

The most important thing that this requires is acceleration of scientific and technical progress. That is what Lenin taught us. In his entire work to direct economic construction, his idea was to rise to the highest levels in science and technology.

The whole world is aware of our country's outstanding successes on this path. But the development of science and technology does not stop. It calls for a further raising of the level and efficiency of scientific research and for rapid use to be made of scientific and technical achievements in the national economy.

The task of improving the organisation of labour and the style of work of all those taking part in social production has also become quite pressing. The main thing here is greater self-exactingness.

Exceptional importance now attaches to the correct organisation of planning. There is no denying, comrades, that many of the complexities we now have to face in the sphere of the economy have their roots in this or that defect in planning, in the imperfection of plans or in their inadequate implementation. That is why one of the most important tasks is continuously to perfect planning methods, and to enhance the scientific, technical and economic validity of current and long-term plans.

May I give a reminder of a call made by Lenin: "Do not be afraid of long-term plans." He himself gave the classic example of such an approach to planning when working on the State Plan for the Electrification of Russia, in which all the calculations and technical grounds were geared to a single goal—the establishment of an advanced power and technical base for the country's economic revival and socialist transformation.

Especially great importance now attaches to improving long-term planning, within the framework of which the available resources and foreseeable requirements are taken into account. Our long-term plans, designed for the solution of fundamental economic and social tasks, must also include our targets and outline the best ways of attaining them, arriving at these by comparing different variants. That is the basis on which it is also possible correctly to determine the concrete tasks which are to be tackled the following year and over the five-year period ahead.

Another important task is planning the allocation of the productive forces in our country, something to which Lenin attached much importance. This involves the most rational, economically efficient development of every area in the light of its concrete conditions.

Long-term plans for the individual branches of our national economy, plans for the solution of major socio-economic problems, consolidated into a single whole, will constitute a general programme for the country's development over a long term. There is no doubt that this approach to planning will produce a considerable effect and will help to accelerate our advance to communism.

Comrades, Lenin saw the construction of a communist economy not only as the concern of economic leaders, and the organisers and commanders of production. He said that "creative activity at the grass roots is the basic factor of the new public life . . . Living, creative socialism is the product of the masses themselves." Accordingly, the Party's course is to ensure the further extension of the working people's participation in running industrial enterprises and state and collective farms, in working for greater efficiency of production, higher labour productivity, the maximum use of the available facilities and the raising of labour discipline.

The Leninist slogan of a regime of economies is not a stop-gap but a constant demand on every member of our socialist society. Our country will become even stronger and richer, and our advance towards communism faster, if we learn to save every minute of our working time, every gramme of raw materials and fuel, every machine part, every hard-earned kopek.

In response to the Party's call, and with the active participation of the trade unions and other social organisations, a country-wide popular movement has now been started to improve the use of reserves in production and tighten the regime of economies in the country. The initiatives of workers, collective farmers, engineers, technicians and administrative personnel and the numerous proposals and concrete obligations being undertaken by the working people are striking evidence of the fact that the working people of town and country, the whole Soviet people are truly aware of being masters of their country, and that they show a personal concern for the interests of production and for the preservation and multiplication of the national wealth. This means, comrades, that we are on the right course. It means that the Soviet people are confidently advancing along the way indicated by Lenin!

It is well known that for our society the fulfilment of economic tasks is not an end in itself but a means. The main purpose and the main meaning of the policy which our Party has been consistently implementing is to create for the working man the most favourable conditions for work, study, leisure and the development and best application of his abilities.

In the last few years we have achieved a great deal in this sphere and have solved a number of major social problems. In that period special attention was devoted to raising the living standards of working people in the lower and middle income brackets in town and country. But we are aware that more big tasks lie ahead of us. Men's needs increase constantly as society and culture develop. Lenin was very well aware of this. He wrote: ". . . When we are showered with new demands from all sides, we say: that is as it should be, that is just what socialism means, when each wants to improve his condition and all want to enjoy the benefits of life."

The task today is not only further to raise remuneration for work but also to expand production of the goods needed by the population, to improve the quality of services, to continue extensive housing construction, and to take fresh measures to protect the health of the working people. Understandably, all these tasks cannot be solved at one go, by the adoption of a resolution, however good. This calls for insistent efforts by the whole Party, by the whole people.

The main thing, comrades, is how much we produce and how, and the attitude we take to work, the main source of our social wealth. There is no need, I think, to argue that one can consume and use only what has been produced, what has been created by man's hands and brain. It is up to the Soviet people themselves to raise their living standards. Today we live as well as we worked yesterday, and tomorrow we shall live as well as we work today.

While devoting maximum attention to economic problems, the Party directs the people's energy to the solution of the whole complex of tasks in communist construction.

We are on the way to gradually overcoming the distinctions between classes and social groups, for which it is necessary, Lenin emphasised, "to abolish . . . the distinction between town and country, as well as the distinction between manual workers and brain workers." It goes without saying that these tasks will be fully solved only in a communist society. But much is already being done to advance in this direction.

The social policy of the Party and the Soviet state is, on the basis of modern science and technology, to more closely approximate the character of the labour of the peasant and that of the worker, to improve living conditions in the countryside and to raise the cultural level of village life. All this in practice results in a gradual eradication of the socio-economic and cultural-welfare distinctions between town and country, between the working class and the peasantry.

At the same time we are gradually overcoming the distinction between workers by hand and by brain. This requires many more steps forward in the development of the economy and culture, an improvement of working conditions and a change in the character of labour, and the further raising of the cultural and professional-technical level of the whole people.

Lenin said that anyone who undertakes the great endeavour of communist construction must understand this: "he can create it only on the basis of modern education, and if he does not acquire this education communism will remain merely a pious wish." We have already done much in the sphere of public education. Almost 80 million, that is, a third of the population, is studying.

However, life does not stand still. We need to go forward, improving the whole system of education in every way. Within a few short years those who are now at school or college will move into production, into science and culture. The progress of our society in the future largely depends on how and what we teach them today. The ancients used to say that the pupil is not a vessel to be filled but a torch to be lit. The task is to teach the young people to think creatively, to prepare them for life, for practical effort.

Comrades, a great achievement of Lenin's is that he worked out the programme for a socialist solution of the national question. This programme has been implemented. The triumph of Lenin's policy on the national question, the Soviet Union's solution of the problem—one of the most acute and most difficult in social life—is an undertaking of tremendous importance, and a major stride forward in mankind's social development.

Communist construction in our multinational country implies the consistent pursuit of the line of bringing the nations together in every way, and strengthening their co-operation and mutual assistance. The way to this is by the further development of the economy and culture in all our Republics, an improvement of mutual exchanges of achievements in material and spiritual culture and, of course, persistent effort to overcome the survivals of nationalism and chauvinism.

Lenin demanded the continuous and tireless education of the working people in the spirit of internationalism, rejecting both great-power chauvinistic and narrowly nationalistic tendencies. He said that "one must *not* think only of one's own nation, but place *above* it the interests of all nations, their common liberty and equality, . . . fight *against* small-nation narrow-mindedness, seclusion and isolation, consider the whole and the general, subordinate the particular to the general interest." The multinational Soviet state founded by Lenin is this whole and this general. Lenin's precept was that we should protect the Union of Soviet Socialist Republics as the apple of our eye. This great precept of Lenin's is being faithfully fulfilled by the Party and the people.

The Soviet socialist state of the whole people is our main instrument in building communism. That is why there is need to constantly strengthen this state and improve the whole system of social administration.

Lenin considered the possibility of involving the working people in the day-to-day administration of the state the greatest advantage of socialism. He set the task of teaching "the people the art of administration." For that purpose we are working and shall continue to work to enhance the role of the Soviets, of social organisations and working people's collectives in the life and development of society, and to improve socialist legislation.

In developing the Soviet state system and socialist democracy, the Party and the Government have been persistently following the Leninist line in improving the state apparatus and making it more efficient. Every stage in the development of the productive forces and of culture, wrote Lenin, must be accompanied by an improvement of our Soviet system.

Lenin wrote that "there can be no victorious socialism that does not practise full democracy." Nor can this be otherwise. The Party has been working steadily and purposefully to develop socialist democracy, which serves above all as a means of drawing millions of working people into the process of conscious historical creative effort and into running the affairs of society and the state.

Our democracy in action is the right of every citizen, every collective and every Republic to take part in deciding questions of social life, combating any departures from the rules and principles of socialist community living, criticising shortcomings and taking an active part in eliminating them. To enable Soviet citizens to enjoy their rights to the fullest, the Party has shown constant concern to improve the forms of popular representation and people's control over the activity of the organs of power and administration.

The broad rights extended by socialist democracy to the working people in various spheres of social life are organically combined with their civic duties. This combination, like the very content of their rights and duties, is determined by the interests of the whole people, the interests of building a communist society.

We regard the development of the Soviet state and socialist democracy above all as a powerful means of attaining our main aim—the building of communism. We shall never agree to the "development of democracy" which is being strongly urged upon us by bourgeois ideologists and their Right-wing opportunist assistants, who show such zeal in trying to recast socialism in their own, bourgeois mould. We have our own, truly democratic traditions, which have stood the test of time. We shall safeguard, preserve, develop and improve these traditions.

No matter how our "adversaries" may wring their hands over the "imperfection" of socialism, no matter what touching concern they may display for its "improvement" and "humanisation," we repeat with pride Lenin's words about proletarian, socialist democracy being a million times more democratic than any bourgeois democracy. Our state was, is and will continue to be a state of the working people, a state for the working people, a state which is governed by the working people.

Following Lenin's path, the Soviet people have created a new, socialist way of life, a new socialist civilisation.

The creative power of socialism, the mobilising power of Lenin's ideas was clearly manifested in the period of preparation for the Lenin centenary. The emulation movement for the fulfilment of the five-year plan ahead of schedule, launched to mark the Lenin anniversary, really has become a movement involving the whole people.

The labour enthusiasm of the people reached its peak in the All-Union Lenin Subbotnik of April 11, which was an unforgettable nationwide festival of inspired labour. Soviet people went to that *subbotnik* with their thoughts on Lenin, on the historical first *subbotnik* which Lenin saw as the Great Beginning of the new, communist attitude to work.

The Central Committee of the CPSU, the Council of Ministers of the USSR and the All-Union Central Council of Trade Unions have taken note of the excellent organisation and high level of activity displayed by all the working people during the All-Union Communist Subbotnik on April 11, and express their deep, heartfelt gratitude to all its participants for their patriotic, selfless and freely given labour effort for the benefit of our socialist country.

It would be impossible to list the labour achievements of the thousands of collectives and of the millions of working people in town and countryside marking the great anniversary. The personnel of many factories and organisations that distinguished themselves in the emulation movement were awarded Lenin centenary diplomas. In honour of the centenary of Lenin's birth workers, collective farmers, brain workers and servicemen were decorated with the jubilee medals "For Meritorious Work" and "For Military Valour." The Central Committee of the Party, the Presidium of the Supreme Soviet of the USSR and the Soviet Government warmly congratulate the valiant working people and servicemen on the award of these high decorations and express the confidence that they will always be in the forefront of the builders of communism.

Allow me, furthermore, to extend heartfelt congratulations to the Lenin Prize winners and all who have been decorated with our country's highest order, which bears the name of Lenin. Honour and glory to them and I wish them further outstanding achievements in promoting the economy, science, technology and culture of our great socialist Motherland.

### 3. Communist Party of the Soviet Union— Party of Lenin

Comrades, our great Party, under whose leadership the Soviet people have won historic victories, was created by Vladimir Ilyich Lenin. He taught the Party to serve the working people with unbounded devotion. He put in its hands a mighty weapon—the theory and policy of struggle against capitalism, of struggle for the revolutionary reconstruction of society, for socialism and communism. "By educating the workers' party," he wrote, ". . . Marxism educates the vanguard of the proletariat, capable of assuming power and *leading the whole people* to socialism, of directing and organising the new system, of being the teacher, the guide, the leader of all the working and exploited people in organising their social life without the bourgeoisie and against the bourgeoisie."

When we re-register the Party membership, Party card No. 1 is always made out in the name of Vladimir Ilyich Lenin. This is not simply a symbol. The great energy of Lenin's mind and the beat of his fiery heart live on in the deeds of the Party. Lenin's ideas, his political steeling and his science of victory are the inexhaustible source from which we draw confidence in our strength and our courage, optimism and will for victory.

Born as the Party of the proletariat, the CPSU has, since the triumph of socialism and, as always, with the support of the working class, become the vanguard of the whole Soviet people. Today approximately one in every eleven citizens of the USSR of the age of 18 or over is a member of the Party. Of the 14 million members of the CPSU more than half are workers or collective farmers. In the Party there are almost 6 million engineers, technicians, agronomists, teachers, doctors and other specialists who are active in the building of communism.

We neither have nor can have another political force that can so fully and consistently take into account, combine and co-ordinate the interests and requirements of all classes and social groups, of all nations and nationalities and of all the generations of our society as the Communist Party is doing. The Party comes forward as the organising core of the entire social system, as the collective brain of the whole Soviet people.

The principal element of the Party's work is its political leadership of society. The tasks of communist construction demand the further improvement of the work of Party and Government organs, the concentration of their attention on pivotal political, economic and ideological problems.

The triumph of socialism, it goes without saying, does not imply the complete and final settlement of all social problems. Like any other developing organism, socialist society is confronted by various difficulties. However, all of them are surmountable. The only thing is not to close our eyes to them but to find effective means of overcoming them. The art of Party and state leadership lies precisely in taking timely note of nascent problems, realistically assessing them and charting the way for solving them. Profoundly and comprehensively studying the situation and the trends of development, courageously laying bare difficulties and contradictions and showing the way to surmount them, the Party blazes the trail of communist construction, setting the people tasks that have to be carried out and inspiring them to perform creative feats of labour.

The deeds of the Leninist Party match its words. The line towards the triumph of the socialist revolution, the line towards socialism, the line towards the building of communism—these are the words of the Party, expressed in its three Programmes. The victory of the October Revolution, the triumph of socialism and the successful advance towards the communist morrow—such is the action of the Party, the action of the whole people.

The Party's strength lies in its fidelity to the principles of Marxism-Leninism, to the principles of proletarian internationalism. Its strength lies in its monolithic unity, which was consolidated and unflaggingly upheld by Lenin. Its strength lies in its unbreakable bond with the working class, with the masses, whose collective leader and organiser it is. Its strength lies in its revolutionary spirit, in its ability critically to assess and profoundly understand the results of its work.

Intrinsic to our Party are a sense of lofty responsibility before the people and high principles. During Lenin's lifetime and after his death the Party courageously and openly criticised, as it continues to do to this day, errors and shortcomings. It sternly denounced the personality cult, which led to violations of the Leninist norms of Party and state life, of socialist legality and democracy. It emphatically rejected subjectivism, which expounds unfounded improvisation in place of a scientific approach to phenomena of social life. The Party tells the people the truth, no matter how stern it may be. ". . . Let us face the truth squarely . . . ," Lenin taught the Communists. "In politics that is always the best and the only correct attitude."

Lenin attached immense significance to developing the political awareness of the masses, which, he wrote, remains "the

basis and chief content of our work." In line with Lenin's precepts the Party is making sure that all Communists consciously
master the fundamentals of Marxism-Leninism and that their
ideological principles find expression in practical participation in the nationwide work of building communism. The
Party educates every Communist and every Soviet citizen as
an ardent patriot who devotes all his strength for the benefit
of the Motherland and, at the same time, as a convinced internationalist.

The importance of educational work among the masses is
particularly great today when a sharp ideological struggle
rages between socialism and capitalism. "We must," Lenin
wrote, "untiringly combat any and every bourgeois ideology,
regardless of the fashionable and striking garb in which it
may drape itself." The bourgeois ideologists and, for that
matter, their accomplices, the revisionists, stand in no need
of borrowing the ability to change garbs and give them a
spurious polish. And it is by no means the goodness of life that
has taught them this. The material from which their garb is
sewn is much too flimsy. The attempts to slander socialism, the
policy of the CPSU and the Soviet Government and, at the
same time, to rehabilitate capitalism and embellish the facade
of its ramshackle edifice fail the test of time.

Nonetheless, the danger of bourgeois ideology and revisionism must on no account be underestimated. Experience shows
that the poisoned seeds of ideological wavering, indifference
to politics and lack of principles sprout on the soil of this sort
of underestimation. Communists are obliged to follow Lenin's
example of political and ideological staunchness, passion in
struggle against any distortion of our revolutionary theory, intolerance of any manifestations of survivals of the old world in
the minds of the citizens of our socialist society.

We live in an age witnessing exceedingly swift development.
Rates of growth are mounting and the scale of communist construction is increasing. Science and Marxist-Leninist theory
are playing an increasingly more important part. The interna-

tional role and responsibility of the Soviet state are growing. All this is enhancing the importance of the Communist Party as the leading force of Soviet society.

Tested and confirmed by the experience of the CPSU, Lenin's teaching that the Party is the leader of the revolutionary masses and the leading force of the new society and Lenin's principles of Party construction are the property not only of the CPSU but also of the fraternal Communist Parties. Facts show that Communists triumph where the Party consistently implements its role as vanguard of the working class and other working people, where the Leninist norms of Party life are strictly observed and where the Party safeguards and tirelessly strengthens its political, organisational and ideological unity. Conversely, any diminution of the Party's role and any departure from the Leninist principles of Party development lead to serious setbacks and may create a threat to the socialist gains of the people.

In order to ensure the success of the great work of building communism the Party must pursue a correct Marxist-Leninist policy, and the broad masses of working people, the whole Soviet people must understand and implement this policy. ". . . We can administer," Lenin said, "only when we express correctly what the people are conscious of. Unless we do this the Communist Party will not lead the proletariat, the proletariat will not lead the masses . . ." The programme of communist construction put forward by the Communist Party has become the vital cause of the whole Soviet people. The Party's unity with the people under the banner of Leninism is the best guarantee that this historic task will be carried out successfully.

Lenin used to say that the Communist Party is the brain, honour and conscience of our epoch. In commemorating the birthday of Lenin we solemnly declare that Soviet Communists will continue doing everything to make our Party, created and reared by Lenin, always worthy of this lofty appraisal of its founder, teacher and leader.

On the Leninist banner of our Party are inscribed the words: "Everything in the name of man, for the sake of man!" The Soviet people will carry this banner along uncharted trails and make our country—the birthplace of socialism—the birthplace of communism, the most humane of social systems.

# III

# LENINISM
# AND THE WORLD
# REVOLUTIONARY PROCESS

Comrades, the period of history that started after the October Revolution was characterised by Lenin as the transition from capitalism to socialism. Lenin was unshakably convinced that the world-wide triumph of socialism was inevitable, that it would come "sooner or later, twenty years earlier or twenty years later," but would definitely come, and that other countries would follow Russia in her advance along the road of building the new society.

The world revolution, Lenin wrote two years after the October Revolution, "judging by its beginning, will continue for many years and will demand much effort." The development of this revolution, he stressed, would not follow the line of an even "maturing" of socialism in the main capitalist countries; its development would, on the whole, be more complicated in view of the contradictory relations within the capitalist world and of the exploitation of some capitalist countries by others, linked with the exploitation of the colonial world. Lenin came to the conclusion that the socialist revolution "will not be solely, or chiefly, a struggle of the revolutionary proletarians in each country against their bourgeoisie—no, it will be a struggle of all the imperialist-oppressed colonies and countries, of all dependent countries, against international imperialism."

It is enough to glance at the world we live in today to become convinced how accurate were Lenin's socio-political analysis and his forecasts based on this analysis, and how fully life has borne out their correctness in all essential features.

However contradictory the picture of the world is today, its main features, its cardinal, decisive trend of development are such as foreseen by Lenin. However much the components of the contemporary world differ from each other, each of them leads to and will ultimately arrive at communism!

## 1. World Socialist System—Vanguard of Mankind's Social Development

It is already a quarter of a century since socialism emerged from the boundaries of one country and became an international force. The socialist revolution was accomplished in a number of countries of Europe and Asia and then spread to the Western Hemisphere as well, triumphing in Cuba.

The world socialist system—the greatest achievement of the working class after the October Revolution—is still very young. However, socialism has become firmly established in the world. It has strikingly shown—not only in the Soviet Union but also in other socialist countries—that it can give a correct answer to the cardinal problems facing mankind, an answer beyond the capability of the capitalist world with its long centuries of experience, an answer that really takes the vital interests of the masses into account.

Historically, as you all know, matters shaped up in such a way that the countries in which the socialist revolution triumphed were not those with the highest level of economic development. But thanks to the new system these countries have made great headway in economic development.

It would be hard to overestimate the impact that has been made on the masses in the rest of the world by the example of the successful development of the new society in a number of countries in different parts of the world, a society without exploitation, without oppression and oppressors, a society administered for the people by the people. This example inspires hundreds of millions of oppressed people and fills them with hope for a happy future.

The very fact of the existence of the socialist world is of immense assistance to the working people in the capitalist countries in their struggle for their rights.

The socialist states have introduced into international life new, unprecedented principles and norms stemming from the ideology of the Communists, from the great and lofty aims of their struggle. The founder of these principles was Lenin, who formulated the fundamentals of socialist foreign policy after the October Revolution.

Lenin always considered the national and international tasks of the socialist state in their indivisible unity. He called upon our Party and people to fight "for a socialist fatherland, for socialism as a fatherland, for the Soviet Republic as a *contingent* of the world army of socialism." The founder of the Soviet state held that in building the new life in its own country it was the duty of the Soviet state to support the revolutionary movement of the proletariat in other countries. He showed us the road to friendship and alliance with the peoples of the colonies and semi-colonies in order to fight international imperialism together with them.

Lenin oriented the Soviet state on a consistent policy of peace in defence of the victorious revolution and the common cause of the working people of all countries. It was no accident that the first act of Soviet power written personally by Lenin was the historic Decree on Peace. It was Lenin who advanced the proposition for "peaceful co-habitation" or, as we now call it, peaceful co-existence of states with different social systems, which, thanks to the consistent policy of the socialist states, has today become one of the cardinal principles underlying international relations. Also on Lenin's initiative one of the very first foreign-policy acts of the Soviet state in the world was to submit a programme for general disarmament and mutually beneficial economic relations with capitalist states.

For more than half a century the Soviet Union's foreign policy has been based on Lenin's ideas and precepts. Written into the decisions of our Party and of the higher organs of the Soviet state they remain the immutable, principled foundation of all the Soviet Union's actions in the international arena. Today, on this great Lenin centenary, we solemnly repeat to the peoples of the whole world:

— True to the behests of the great Lenin, the Union of Soviet Socialist Republics shall continue to do everything in its power to enable the peoples of the socialist countries to live in peace and peacefully carry out the great work of building the new society, and to steadfastly strengthen the position of world socialism and the close cooperation and militant unity of the socialist states.

— The countries pursuing an anti-imperialist policy and the peoples fighting for freedom, against imperialist aggression, shall always have in the person of our country a reliable and true friend and ally.

— Realistically-minded circles in the bourgeois countries, circles that really recognise the principles of peaceful co-existence, may be confident that in the Soviet Union they will have a partner prepared to promote mutually beneficial cooperation.

— We shall continue our active efforts to halt the arms race, which is ruinous to the peoples, to secure disarmament and get outstanding issues between states settled on a reasonable foundation, by negotiation.

Socialist in content, the Leninist foreign policy of the Soviet state is consistently internationalist, genuinely democratic and profoundly peace-loving. It is one of the major sources of the strength and world-wide prestige of our socialist Motherland and world socialism. This is a powerful weapon and we shall make the utmost use of it in our struggle for peace and communism.

The principles of socialist foreign policy formulated by

Lenin have now become the foundation of the foreign policy line of a whole group of countries belonging to the world socialist system.

The whole of mankind's greatest blessing is the fact that the united might of the socialist countries and their active policy in defence of peace fetter the aggressive ambitions of the imperialists and create a decisive obstacle to the unleashing of a world nuclear rocket war by the aggressors. This result of the policy pursued by the socialist countries benefits all mankind.

Where the imperialists nonetheless take the road of military adventures against a socialist country or have recourse to "quiet" counter-revolution they feel the strength and solidarity of the socialist states.

Comrades, look what is happening to the US aggression against the Democratic Republic of Vietnam and the people of South Vietnam. No social system but socialism could have given the liberation struggle of the Vietnamese people such a scale, such organisation, staunchness and tenacity. No political force but the Marxist-Leninist Party could have armed a fighting people with such a lucid understanding of the aims of the struggle and inspired them to the performance of a mass feat. As a result of the heroism of the Vietnamese patriots multiplied by the might of socialist solidarity and by broad assistance from the Soviet Union and other socialist countries, the US adventure in Vietnam is suffering failure. The feat of Vietnam will go down in history. Honour and glory to the heroic Vietnamese people!

Similarly instructive is the failure of the anti-socialist conspiracy in Czechoslovakia. This was a long-premeditated, demagogy-screened attempt of the remnants of the former exploiting classes in alliance with the Right-wing opportunists and with the support of world imperialism to destroy the foundations of the socialist system in Czechoslovakia, isolate her from the fraternal countries and thereby strike a heavy blow at the positions of socialism in Europe. But the staunchness of the Marxist-Leninist core of the Czechoslovak Communist Party and determined action by Czechs and Slovaks devoted to the cause of socialism and by allied countries loyal to the principles of socialist internationalism frustrated the dangerous plans of enemies aimed against the common interests of socialism and, in the long run, against peace in the European continent. This was further proof of the great significance of the internationalist solidarity of the socialist countries. Today our friends and our enemies have no doubt about the efficacy of its strength, and that is very good.

Comrades, each of the independent countries in the world socialist system has accomplished the transition from capitalism to socialism in its own way and resolves a number of tasks of socialist construction, common to all, by its own specific methods.

Lenin foresaw this diversity of "ways, methods and means of moving to the common goal." As early as 1916 he formulated his famous conclusion on this question: "All nations," he wrote, "will arrive at socialism—this is inevitable, but all will do so in not exactly the same way, each will contribute something of its own to some form of democracy, to some variety of the dictatorship of the proletariat, to the varying rate of socialist transformations in the different aspects of social life."

That is what has actually taken place. The uniqueness of the concrete historical situation, the diversity of local conditions and the different and sometimes more or less successful approaches to the solution of some problems of socialist construction have given rise to a number of features in the development of individual socialist countries. However, these are features within the framework of a single, common process developing under identical laws. Local conditions are taken into consideration in the building of socialism not for the sake of splintering the common revolutionary front but of attaining the common goal more surely and effectively and hastening the triumph of the new system and uniting the socialist forces of different countries. That is how this problem was understood by Lenin, who was a confirmed internationalist. That is how it is understood by the Communists of the socialist countries, who are continuing Lenin's work.

Historical experience has clearly borne out Lenin's proposition that the different features in the development of the socialist countries ". . . can apply only to what is of lesser importance." The main thing is that the road to socialism and the system itself are characterised, as is emphasised by the fraternal Parties, by a number of fundamental laws that are inherent in the socialist society of any country.

Experience shows that *the road of different countries to socialism* is marked by such major common milestones as the socialist revolution in one form or another, including the smashing and replacement of the state machine of the exploiters; the establishment of one or another form of the dictatorship of the proletariat in alliance with other strata of the working people, and the abolition of the exploiting classes; the socialisation of the means of production and the consolidation of socialist relations of production and other social relations in town and countryside; the bringing of cultural values within the reach of the masses of working people, i.e., the cultural revolution in Lenin's meaning of the word.

On the other hand, when we speak of the main features of *socialism that has been built,* this question is likewise clear to Communists. It is clear to us today not only from the theoretical propositions of Marxist teaching but also from the experience of development gained by the socialist countries. What are these features? They are the power of the working people with the vanguard role exercised by the working class and the leadership of social development provided by the Marxist-Leninist Party; public ownership of the means of production and, on its basis, the planned development of the national economy on the highest technological level for the benefit of the whole people; the implementation of the principle "from each according to his ability, to each according to his work"; the education of the whole people in the spirit of the ideology of scientific communism, in a spirit of friendship with the peoples of the fraternal socialist countries and the working people of the whole world; and lastly, a foreign policy founded on the principles of proletarian, socialist internationalism.

All these general, basic elements of socialism are of decisive significance.

The development and strengthening of the world socialist system are the most valuable contribution of the peoples of the socialist countries to the common revolutionary cause of Communists and the anti-imperialist struggle of the masses throughout the world. Imperialism is waging a dogged, savage struggle in various forms against the world socialist system. It seeks to hinder its economic growth, restrict its influence over the peoples of the world, poison it ideologically and split and isolate it politically. For that reason the recent International Meeting of fraternal Parties put forward in its Main Document the exceedingly important proposition: "The defence of socialism is the internationalist duty of Communists."

Comrades, the task of *strengthening the unity and promoting all-round co-operation among the socialist countries* is becoming particularly pressing and important today.

The victory of socialism in a number of countries has made it possible to establish between them relations of a new type—fraternal relations based on the principles of socialist internationalism. Genuine equality and respect for each other's independence and sovereignty are combined in these relations with comradely mutual assistance, socialist solidarity and a joint struggle for common aims and ideals.

However, experience shows that these relations between socialist countries do not take shape automatically; to mould and develop them and surmount the difficulties and contradictions that sometimes arise, the socialist states and their ruling Parties have to pursue a principled, internationalist policy.

Regrettably, we sometimes get cases of co-operation between socialist countries being disrupted in a most serious manner. This is shown, for instance, by the present state of China's relations with the Soviet Union and other socialist countries. This situation is obviously the result of the nationalistic policy of the Chinese leadership and its rupture with the principles laid down by Lenin.

Today, as we mark the Lenin jubilee, I should like to recall the attitude of Sun Yat-sen, the great Chinese revolutionary and democrat, to Lenin and his teaching. This is what he said:

"In the course of the many centuries of world history there have been thousands of leaders and scholars with eloquent words on their lips that were never translated into reality. You, Lenin, are the exception. You not only spoke and taught, but translated your words into reality. You created a new country. You showed us the road of joint struggle. On your road you have encountered thousands of obstacles, which I am encountering on my road. I want to follow your road, and although my enemies are against this, my people will laud me for it."

These are fine words, comrades! It is precisely by jointly following the road charted by Lenin, by waging a joint struggle against the sinister forces of imperialist reaction, for the triumph of the sacred cause of socialism and communism that the correct prospect is opened for the future development of relations between China and the Soviet Union, and between China and other socialist countries.

Practice shows that nothing good comes of a departure from socialist internationalism, from its replacement by nationalism and chauvinism. Such a policy, naturally, does not conform either to the interests of the world socialist system as a whole, or to the interests of the revolutionary process throughout the world. But it is fully in line with interests of the imperialists, who are delighted by every sign of a weakening of the unity of the socialist countries and are prepared to help to shake this unity in every way they can.

The enemies of socialism are the only ones who benefit by the virulent anti-Soviet campaign that has been conducted in China during the past few years. Lately it has been carried on under the screen of an alleged threat from the Soviet Union. By their actions against the country of Lenin and against the world communist movement the initiators of this campaign expose themselves before the masses as apostates of the revolutionary cause of Lenin.

As regards the Soviet Union, we take a resolute stand for socialist internationalism and the restoration of good relations between socialist countries wherever they have been broken. We shall not be found wanting. The Central Committee of the CPSU and the Soviet Government shall continue to work actively and consistently in this direction in a Leninist way.

Lenin tirelessly emphasised the vital importance of unity, the need for close and all-sided fraternal co-operation among peoples who have taken the road to socialism. We Soviet Communists are true to Lenin's behests. We are doing, as we always have done, everything in our power to promote political and economic co-operation among socialist states and their ideological unity.

On this point Lenin wrote: "We . . . who are faced by a huge front of imperialist powers, we, who are fighting imperialism, represent an alliance that requires close military unity, and any attempt to violate this unity we regard as absolutely impermissible, as a betrayal of the struggle against international imperialism." To this day we regard these words as a sacred behest to all contingents of the socialist front fighting imperialism in the Leninist way. Remembering these words, we shall bend every effort to make the Warsaw Treaty Organisation, the military alliance of the socialist countries, still more powerful and to strengthen the joint defence capability of the socialist states.

The historical role played today by the world socialist system, vanguard of mankind's social development, is great and lofty. It has entered our complex and turbulent epoch as the embodiment of the age-old dream of the working people and exploited masses of all countries, as a sentence passed on the forces of reaction, oppression and aggression, as the mighty bulwark of all fighters for freedom, independence and lasting peace, as a symbol of hope and an earnest of the future happiness of all peoples. For a Communist today, for every person who is true to the teaching and cause of the great Lenin, no duty is higher than that of contributing to the further development of the world socialist system, to the cause of strengthening its might, cohesion and unity.

## 2. Leninism—Victorious Banner of the Struggle for the Liberation of Peoples

When Lenin analysed the new phenomena in capitalist society he defined not only the main features of imperialism as the monopoly stage of capitalism, but also the direction of its development. Bourgeois society, he pointed out, was moving "from monopoly to etatisation," that is to say, to state-monopoly capitalism. He precisely defined imperialism's historical place as the *last stage* of capitalism, as the "threshold of socialism."

Imperialism is moving exactly in the direction foreseen by Lenin. The general crisis of capitalism as a world system continues to deepen. Today, more than ever before, imperialism is a world of the omnipotence of colossal monopolies, which continue to grow in size. The main weapon for preserving the class rule of the bourgeoisie today has become the merging of the forces of the monopolies with the power of the state in a single mechanism of struggle against the world of socialism, against the working class and the general democratic movement of the masses. Lenin's characteristic of the political substance of imperialism, which he expressed in the laconic but meaningful formula of "reaction all along the line," has also been confirmed.

The peoples of the world are beginning to see more and more clearly that imperialism, which has already forced two world wars on mankind, is in our days inseparable from such crimes as wars of aggression, flagrant interference in the life of other countries and peoples, and the brutality of racists and colonialists. In different parts of the world it maintains outworn political regimes that are hated by the peoples. Imperialism gave birth to fascism, a monstrous embodiment of obscurantism and reaction. Militarism, which has penetrated all the pores of social life in the bourgeois countries, has attained unparalleled proportions.

The peoples of the world are seeing with increasing clarity that imperialism has created a vast production machine but that this machine serves only to increase the wealth and power of a tiny handful of capitalist magnates. In the sphere ruled by world capitalism tens and hundreds of millions are suffering from hunger and poverty. Imperialism uses the greatest achievements of technology to intensify the exploitation of millions of working people and to prepare for piratical wars. Mankind pays for the existence of imperialism with hundreds of thousands of lives—the victims of these wars and the victims of ruthless exploitation.

Lastly, what prospects does this inhuman system hold out for the ordinary man? Only one thing: more blood and sweat, more prisoners in the jails, more maimed and killed, and a still greater menace to the very existence of entire nations. Modern capitalism is a society without ideals, a society without a future. Hence its moral disintegration, spiritual hollowness and stupefying philistinism that is encouraged by a philistine pseudo-culture specially created for this purpose. Hence the monstrous crime wave in the Western countries, the black torrents of drug addiction and pornography, and the sea of perverted feelings and mutilated souls.

Lenin's wrathful words unmasking imperialism resound with renewed force today. "On all sides, at every step," he wrote in 1913, "one comes across problems which man is quite capable of solving *immediately*, but capitalism is in the way. It has amassed enormous wealth—and has made men the *slaves* of this wealth . . .

"Civilisation, freedom and wealth under capitalism call to mind the rich glutton who is rotting alive but will not let what is young live on." The whole image of modern capitalist society, comrades, serves as the most convincing testimony of the consummate accuracy of this characteristic given by Lenin.

Naturally, all this does not mean that we can forget or belittle the menace harboured by imperialism. Imperialism will not collapse by itself, automatically. No, it is still strong. Active and determined action by all the revolutionary forces is needed to overthrow it.

Such forces exist. The front of their struggle is growing steadily broader.

In line with Lenin's behests, the Meeting of Communist and Workers' Parties put forward an extensive militant programme of struggle against imperialism under present-day conditions. The majority of the working people of the non-socialist world have joined in this struggle. In the front ranks is the revolutionary vanguard of the working class consisting of conscious fighters for socialism. But far from everybody has the same clear understanding of the general meaning and end purpose of the struggle. Millions are rising because they can no longer endure ruthless exploitation. Millions are joining the battle for elementary human rights, for the freedom and independence of their enslaved people. Others, and their numbers are steadily growing in all parts of the world, are demanding with anxiety and anger in their hearts an end to the bloodthirsty adventures of the imperialist aggressors, to their insane policy of building up armaments, the stockpiles of which are already today capable of bringing death to hundreds of millions of people. Imperialism is being dealt increasingly more telling blows in the principal centres of its rule and on its flanks by the peoples it is oppressing and exploiting.

During the past few years the struggle of the working masses in the capitalist countries has acquired such a scale and intensity that one can justifiably say that a new political situation is taking shape there. The huge wave of strikes and political battles of millions of working people in France in the summer of 1968, the unparalleled general strike of 20 million workers in Italy last November, and the annual militant marches of millions of Japanese workers are striking indications of the social storm brewing in the world of imperialism. But is that all? In Spain and Argentina, in Chile and Uruguay, in the USA, West Germany and Sweden, in fact, everywhere, the bourgeoisie feels the mounting blows of the working-class movement. Everywhere the trade unions are growing more active and increasing the scale of their activity. An extremely important element is that today this struggle is waged by no means solely under economic slogans. It is increasingly becoming a political struggle of the working class, a struggle for social rights and democratic freedoms, a struggle against the omnipotence of the monopolies.

These militant actions of tens of millions of proletarians are the best reply to the specious fabrications of the enemies of Leninism, who assert that the working class of the capitalist countries has "lost" its revolutionary spirit. No, the militant spirit of the international proletariat has not faded. And the bourgeoisie is feeling this in a most tangible manner.

The blows being struck at imperialism by the masses are growing increasingly more powerful. This is an indisputable fact. But Communists assess the situation soberly. They know that the bourgeoisie still succeeds in holding a considerable section of the masses, including a section of the working class, captive to reactionary or reformist ideology. However, the consciousness that the present practices can no longer be tolerated is growing not only among the advanced section of the proletariat but also among other strata of the people.

Lenin taught the Communists that at sharp turns in social development it is exceedingly important to find and correctly determine the proper path or "special turn of events" that can make the masses understand the main thing, which is that a determined revolutionary struggle has to be waged for the overthrow of the capitalist system.

Of key importance today is Lenin's conclusion that in the epoch of imperialism the tasks of the struggle for democracy and the struggle for socialism draw ever closer and merge into a common torrent. It is precisely in line with this that today the Communist Parties of the bourgeois countries are putting forward programmes of struggle for democracy on the basis of which the masses can be rallied round the working class and led to the next stage, namely, the struggle for socialism. This strategy fully conforms to the considerations put forward by Lenin. In *The Impending Catastrophe and How to Combat It*, written in 1917, he pointed out that the struggle for far-reaching democratic reforms could lead to the creation of a revolutionary-democratic state in which the foundations of the rule of the big capitalists would be radically undermined. This, he wrote, "will *still not* be socialism, but it will *no longer* be capitalism. It will be a tremendous *step towards* socialism."

But whatever stages of transition the revolutionary masses will have to go through and whatever intermediate programmes and slogans the Communists put forward to rally these masses they always remember that ahead of them is the last and decisive battle, the battle for the overthrow of capitalism, the battle for socialism. Communists are what they are because they subordinate their entire struggle to this main, end goal. For the sake of this goal they rally round the working class more and more contingents of fighters. For the sake of this goal they tirelessly work to unite the working class itself, against all splitters of every hue—from the Right-wing leaders of the Social Democratic Parties to the exponents of "Left" adventurism.

It goes without saying that life may introduce its amendments into the plans of struggle drawn up beforehand, into the planned stages of its development. This is all the more true in our days when more and more strata of the population whose actions are sometimes spontaneous, are being drawn into the political struggle. Unexpected turns in the course of events are possible. For that reason Lenin's appeal that they be prepared for any change in the situation, for the use of any forms of struggle—peaceful and non-peaceful, legal and illegal—is particularly topical for Communists today. Armed with the all-conquering teaching of Marx, Engels and Lenin, the Communists of the capitalist countries bear this in mind. True sons and reliable vanguard of their peoples, they are forming the masses into the army of the revolution. There is no doubt whatever that the coming years will witness further powerful blows by this army at imperialism, a fortress that is still dangerous but doomed by history.

A vast part of the world today consists of former colonies of the imperialist powers whose peoples won state independence during the past few decades as a result of a long and determined heroic struggle. New turbulent processes are taking place in these countries. And the great Leninist teaching gives the only true key to understanding these processes.

The speech made by Lenin at the Third Congress of the Comintern in 1921 contained the following stirring words: "It is perfectly clear that in the impending decisive battles in the world revolution," he said, "the movement of the majority of the population of the globe, initially directed towards national liberation, will turn against capitalism and imperialism and will, perhaps, play a much more revolutionary part than we expect."

That is exactly what is happening today.

The liquidation of the colonial empires was a most powerful blow at imperialism. However, the imperialists have not laid down their arms. Today they seek to facilitate the development of capitalist orders in the former colonial countries, feeling that by employing more "flexible" and cunning methods it will be easier to rob them in the present conditions. In this lies the purport of neo-colonialism. But it would be wrong to think that the policy of the present-day colonialists has become harmless, and that their hands are any cleaner than they were before. By no means. Where they feel it necessary the imperialists continue to shed the blood of freedom-loving peoples without the least compunction, flagrantly interfering in the internal affairs of the young states, weaving webs of intrigue against progressive leaders, and organising conspiracies and coups in order to remove governments that do not suit them.

The number of examples of this policy is more than sufficient. The aggression in Southeast Asia, the intrigues in Cyprus, plotting in India and in African countries—everywhere one sees the bloody tracks of the imperialists and their hostile activity against the peoples.

This same line can be seen in the Middle East as well. The real goal of the Israeli aggression and of the policy pursued by the US imperialist circles backing it is to abolish the progressive regimes in the UAR, Syria and a number of other Arab countries and to ensure conditions for the unhindered exploitation of the oil and other wealth of the Arab East by foreign monopolies.

But powerful popular forces are now rising against the conspiracies of the imperialists. The Arab peoples are actively and staunchly defending their just cause. On their side are the Soviet Union and other socialist countries, and the communist and democratic movements of the whole world. One can confidently say that the cause of the imperialists is doomed and that the cause of the freedom of peoples is unconquerable!

Life is thus clearly showing that the further development of the liberated countries along the road of national independence inevitably leads to a clash with the policy of imperialism and can only progress in struggle against imperialist policy.

Today with the disintegration of the colonial empire of the capitalists in the main completed, the former colonial world has entered a new stage: *the struggle no longer solely for national but also—and this is now the main thing—for social liberation is today becoming more and more sharply pronounced.* The young countries are looking for ways of development without the capitalists, without exploitation of man by man.

Lenin charted a clear-cut prospect of possible development of economically backward countries along a non-capitalist road, i.e., in the direction of socialism without passing through the stage of capitalism. This forecast has been borne out. During the past few years quite a large group of liberated countries have started serious and far-reaching reforms in all spheres of social life, proclaiming the building of socialism as their end goal. This is, of course, not easy for the young states, whose development had been held up for centuries by the colonialists. For this it is necessary to raise the productive forces to the level required by socialism, establish totally new relations of production, change the psychology of the people and set up a new administrative apparatus relying on the support of the masses. This road of development, as Lenin said, must include a whole series of "gradual preliminary stages," of "special transitional measures."

The implementation of all these tasks requires extensive and persevering work by the entire people, by the workers, peasants and intelligentsia led by the vanguard which clearly sees the socialist goals and the road to them. Of particular importance here is the unity of all progressive, democratic forces without exception. The peoples of the countries that have chosen the non-capitalist road of development have enthusiastically embarked on this great work for they know that it is being done for the benefit of all the working people, for the sake of the genuine independence and prosperity of the beloved Homeland. Their task is today made easier by the fact that they can rely on the support of sincere friends—the socialist countries and other progressive, anti-imperialist states, and also the international communist and working-class movement.

Lenin attached enormous importance to the formation of an alliance between the socialist world and the peoples of colonial countries who have awakened to active political struggle. This alliance has now become a reality.

As regards the Soviet Union and its Communist Party, they faithfully fulfil Lenin's behest that the utmost support should be rendered to the liberation movement of the peoples.

The genuinely friendly relations permeated with a spirit of mutual trust and respect that have taken shape between us and many countries of the former colonial world are concrete embodiment of this line of our policy. Allow me, comrades, from this rostrum to address the peoples and leaders of the liberated countries on behalf of the Soviet people and convey to them our warmest and most sincere wishes for success in their difficult but glorious struggle!

An important feature of the present stage of world development is that today the international communist movement plays a vastly enhanced role in the life of the peoples and in the struggle to solve the basic problems worrying the whole of mankind.

We Communists are proud that the great Lenin stood at the cradle of our movement. In the course of the half century that has elapsed it has become the most influential political force in the world. The successes of the communist movement are unquestionable. But we do not forget that the summits it has achieved today were reached by tremendous effort and unceasing struggle, and at the price of many, many sacrifices. No fighters for the happiness of the working people are more dedicated than the glorious cohort of Marxists-Leninists. From generation to generation their names will be handed down as an example of real heroism, as a symbol of unshakable belief that a bright future lies before mankind. Honour and glory to the heroes of the communist movement, the Prometheans of our epoch!

Comrades, it is obvious to us that Communists can successfully carry out the tasks confronting them only if they come forward as a united and cemented international force. We always remember the behest of the great Lenin, who taught that a firm international alliance of revolutionaries-internationalists is the guarantee of the victory of the liberation movement of the working class. An important landmark in the struggle to strengthen this alliance was last year's International Meeting of Communist and Workers' Parties.

Many obstacles still stand in the way of the implementation of the internationalist line of uniting the fraternal Parties.

"Communists," Lenin wrote, "are in duty bound not to gloss over shortcomings in their movement, but to criticise them openly so as to remedy them the more speedily and radically." True to this behest of the leader, we have to say today that certain weaknesses and difficulties have manifested themselves in the communist movement over the past few years, disrupting its unity in a number of links and preventing Communists from making full use of the possibilities of the revolutionary struggle. This concerns the policy of the "Left" opportunists, including the Trotskyites, who seek to replace the scientifically substantiated Marxist line of the revolutionary movement by adventurism. This also concerns manifestations of a Right deviation which tries to emasculate Lenin's teaching of its revolutionary substance. One of the features of the present stage of the revolutionary struggle is that in many cases both Right and "Left" opportunism intertwine with nationalistic trends.

In the present epoch, when the international class struggle has grown extremely acute, the danger of Right and "Left" deviations and of nationalism in the communist movement has grown more tangible than ever before. The struggle against Right and "Left" opportunism and nationalism cannot, therefore, be conducted as a campaign calculated for only some definite span of time. The denunciation of opportunism of all kinds was and remains an immutable law for all Marxist-Leninist Parties. Lenin emphasised that "the fight against imperialism is a sham and humbug unless it is inseparably bound up with the fight against opportunism."

Imperialist ideologists and politicians have started intensive subversive activities against the Communists. They are using every possible means and method to weaken the unity of the communist front and drive a wedge where the slightest cracks begin to show. All this requires an intensification of the active offensive struggle of Communists against bourgeois ideology and still more active co-operation among them on a world scale. All this demands the unity of the working-class and national-liberation movements with the peoples of the socialist countries building the new society.

The entire experience accumulated by our movement shows that provided the Communists pursue a correct policy no objective circumstances or reasons will of themselves automatically lead to a disruption of our unity. In this sense a huge and truly historic responsibility devolves on all Marxists-Leninists.

The world revolutionary process is developing inexorably. The stronger and more influential the Marixist-Leninist Parties become, the greater will be the achievements of this process. The deeper the great ideas of Marxism-Leninism sink into the minds of the masses, the sooner will the revolution achieve new victories. Under the banner of Leninism we shall secure the complete triumph of our just cause.

*　*　*

Comrades, today when the entire course of social development inexorably hastens the downfall of capitalism, Lenin's words that Marxism raises questions "not only in the sense of explaining the past but also in the sense of a bold forecast of the future and of bold practical action for its achievement" resound with particular force. While being occupied with the present and working on contemporary day-to-day problems, we compare our actions with our ideals, with immediate and distant prospects of social development. We think of and build the future.

Our ideas of the future stem from the scientific principles of Marxism-Leninism. Our knowledge of these principles and unbounded faith in the revolutionary, creative possibilities of the working people fill us with optimism.

Naturally, nobody can foretell in detail the course of events at any moment of future development. But if we approach the problem not from the standpoint of details or fortuities, which are always possible, if, as Lenin put it, "the matter is taken on a broad scale, then particular and trifling details recede into the background and the chief motive forces of world history become apparent." And since the main motive forces of world history are known and since the principal trends of historical development have been brought to light, it becomes obvious that the struggle between the two world systems will ultimately end with the triumph of communism on a global scale.

While showing the peoples of the world the majestic prospect of a communist future, the only real prospect that conforms to the basic interests of all peoples, Marxists-Leninists are not inclined to simplify the tasks involved. The road to communism is a road of long and persevering struggle. The peoples will have to surmount the fierce resistance of the old, outworn world.

But the matter does not end there. To build communism means to reconstruct the whole life of society on a foundation that differs fundamentally from capitalism. This means uprooting the habits and traditions formed in the course of the millennia of exploiting society—private-ownership psychology and morals, and distrust between peoples of different nations and races.

Our confidence that all these difficult tasks will be successfully carried out is not solely the result of a theoretical analysis. It is founded on the irrefutable facts of 20th century history, in the course of which more than one-third of mankind has won liberation from the yoke of capitalism. It is founded on the experience of the truly grandiose changes that have taken place and continue to take place in the socialist countries. It is founded on our own experience—the experience of the country that was the first in the world to start the practical building of communism. In carrying out the programme charted by the Party, Soviet people are by their tireless work and heroic efforts blazing the path which will sooner or later be followed by the working people of all countries. Every success and every victory won by us bring nearer the hour when all mankind will break the social and moral chains of the past and enter a new world, the world of communism.

But no matter to what summits mankind ascends it will always remember that the gigantic figure of Lenin, thinker and revolutionary, stood at the sources of communist civilisation. Nothing is more sacred to a Communist, to a Leninist, than to devote all his strength, intelligence and will to bring nearer the future for which Lenin fought.

Comrades, I should like to end my speech with the wise words of Lenin: "The whole point is not to rest content with the skill we have acquired by previous experience, but *under all circumstances to go on, under all circumstances to strive for something bigger,* under all circumstances to proceed from simpler to more difficult tasks. Otherwise," Lenin taught us, "no progress whatever is possible and in particular no progress is possible in socialist construction." We Communists shall go farther. We shall strive for something bigger. And no matter how difficult the tasks that confront and will confront us may be, we shall carry them out. The world Lenin dreamed of shall be built!

# Part II

SPEECH AT THE 16TH CONGRESS OF THE LENINIST
YOUNG COMMUNIST LEAGUE OF THE SOVIET UNION

Dear comrade delegates,

Dear members of the YCL,

The Congress of the Leninist Young Communist League is a great event in the life of Soviet young people and in the entire socio-political life of the country.

The Central Committee of our Party authorized me to convey to the delegates and the guests of the 16th Congress of the All-Union Leninist Young Communist League and to all the young Leninists of the country cordial greetings from the Communists of the Soviet Union and to wish you success in your work.

Only a month ago we celebrated the birth centenary of Vladimir Ilyich Lenin. Lenin is the eternal ideal of man, fighter and political leader for Soviet young men and women and for progressive young people everywhere in the world.

Marx wrote that history recognized the greatness of those who, while working for the common weal, themselves became more noble and that experience hails as the happiest, the one who brought joy to the greatest number of people. Young Vladimir Ulyanov chose this ideal. Lenin's influence upon the destinies of mankind is tremendous and immeasurable. The revolutionary transformation of the world, to which he had devoted his life, is tremendous and immeasurable. History justly calls the age of the Great October Revolution the age of Lenin.

Our people have scored genuinely great victories under the banner of Lenin. But Lenin taught us not to rest content with our successes, soberly to appraise what we have accomplished and to focus attention mainly on the unsolved questions. Permit me to wish your Congress, too, to proceed in a spirit of thorough exactingness when discussing problems of concern to young people, and to outline the plans of work of the Komsomol for the near future in a Leninist, businesslike manner.

Here are assembled representatives of the glorious multinational army of the young fighters for communism. Today, there are 27,000,000 in the ranks of the Leninist Komsomol. 27,000,-000, and not several hundred thousand, as was the case half a century ago, when Vladimir Ilyich made his historic speech at the 3rd Congress of the YCL.

When one looks at this hall sparkling with young faces, one cannot but think of what makes you kindred to those fellows and girls who heard Lenin and who made a great contribution to the victory of socialism and the defence of its gains. You are just as passionately loyal to the cause of communism, just as prepared for self-sacrifice for the common cause, just as irreconcilable towards imperialists, and you have the same feeling of class proletarian solidarity with the millions of toilers all over the world.

Yes, you are just like they were in substance, in that which constitutes the essence of Soviet character. And in the things that distinguish you—education, culture—you owe all that to your fathers and grandfathers who paved your way into the future.

The young people highly value the exploit of their fathers. But selflessness, enthusiasm, loyalty to ideals and a readiness to perform feats is just as necessary today as in the past. You are destined to defend what your fathers had won, and to implement the grandiose plans of communist construction. It is an honourable, responsible and inspiring task. And believe me, the time will come when your children and grandchildren will envy the deeds and accomplishments of the young people of the '70s.

Time dictates its laws to people. The young inherit from the old. That is what happens in the family. And that is what happens in society. The change of generations includes joint work by people of different ages, work hand in hand and side by side. The time comes for every generation to emerge to key positions in the life of society. This time is setting in for you, too. The older comrades have faith in you and expect of you new heroic deeds and new labour victories.

We cannot make successful progress in the socio-political life of the country without the participation of young people. The Soviet Komsomol is a tremendous force. Today it unites in its ranks workers, students, collective farmers, scientists, cosmonauts and teachers.

As was stressed in the message of greetings of the Central Committee of the Communist Party of the Soviet Union to your Congress, which was published today, the Party highly values the wonderful deeds of the Komsomol, of Soviet young people, and their selfless labour for the benefit of our great Motherland. The Party is vitally interested in the all-round development of the social and political activities of the young people, and it continues to assign to the Komsomol the solution of problems on a national scale. The Komsomol of today can cope with the most complex and most responsible assignments!

Comrades, you, of course, will discuss on which sections of communist construction it is most expedient to concentrate the effort of the Komsomol today. I would like to express a few considerations on this.

As you are aware, Soviet economy is entering a new important stage. The technical basis of industry and agriculture is being radically changed. All this introduces much that is new in our approach to the solution of economic problems, and to the working out and implementation of our economic and technical policies. Practically all the more or less major problems of our social development are connected today with scientific and technological progress.

We might say that at the time of NEP, and of the first five-year plans, we went to the primary school of socialist economic management. Today we are faced by higher-school problems of socialist economy. These are the most complex and the most creative tasks on the road to communism. You, YCLers, will also be coping with them under the leadership of the Party. But to be able to achieve success in that and not to lag behind the age, not to lag behind the rates of the scientific and technological progress, the main thing is to master knowledge. Lenin's demand ". . . first, to learn, secondly, to learn, and thirdly, to learn . . ." remains as before the indispensable rule of life.

The Party takes care that the young builders of communism shall be well educated and creatively thinking people. The young people must clearly realize that science and technology have no limits in their progress. Therefore, it is necessary to foster in oneself an unquenchable thirst for knowledge, and lively responsiveness to new scientific and technical discoveries, while still studying at school.

Today, after the measures adopted by the Party and the Government, even more young people come to the universities and institutes from industrial enterprises. A considerable number of young people from collective and state farms have been added to our establishments of higher learning. The Komsomol has "adopted" these young people, and helps them in their studies. This, comrades, is a good thing, and necessary.

The concern displayed by the Komsomol for the development of the scientific-engineering activities of young working people also merits all-round support. Professional competitions have become traditional. Young turners, tractor-drivers, builders, milling-machine operators, dairy maids and cooks compete in demonstrating their skill and in their working know-how. Hundreds of thousands of young men and women take part in the work of students' scientific societies and voluntary design bureaus. Many bright talents are also discovered at the exhibitions of the engineering activities of young people.

Our agriculture is an important field of activities for the young enthusiasts of scientific and technological progress. It goes without saying that only people technically educated, well qualified and fond of the soil and of the work on it, can cope with the major tasks placed by the Party before our agriculture. We stress with satisfaction that the Komsomol responded actively to the Party's appeal to help the rural young people in mastering the engineering professions, which our countryside needs so much.

The entire variegated and many-sided activities of the young rationalizers, inventors, and innovators of production—these genuine torchbearers of engineering progress—mould a new type of working man—a proponent of everything progressive. The introduction of new progressive ideas always reveals wonderful scientific and organizational talents and fosters a high degree of strictness and a feeling of civil responsibility in people. We need people precisely with such qualities.

The alliance of science, engineering and production is the token of our successes. At a time of development of the scientific and technological revolution it is up to you, comrades, to expand and to strengthen this alliance. It is the task of the Komsomol to seek ever new ways of drawing all young men and women into this most important work.

The Komsomol has always proved by deeds its ability to concentrate the efforts of young people on the main trends. We highly value the YCL's "adoption" of the key projects in our industrial construction. Honour and praise to the Komsomol for this.

It is necessary, however, that the young people should work with enthusiasm everywhere, in all the vitally important branches of our tremendous socialist economy. We usually say of the people who build industrial enterprises, extract coal and oil, lay roads and produce modern machinery and equipment, that they are in the front lines of communist construction. But the work done by those who build housing, produce consumer goods and work in the services industry, is no less important for society. And as for romantic appeal, it is to be found in any important job which is necessary for the people. Romantic enthusiasm always accompanies those who are capable of looking in a new way at their work, and of offering a new and a better solution.

In other words, the Komsomol organizations should keep within their field of vision the entire range of tasks which are posed by life, whether they be brilliant and impressive, or merely routine ones, which might seem to be of secondary importance at first glance.

I should like to draw your attention to such an important economic problem as the need for further economizing, and of improving the utilization of production reserves.

The Soviet people have built up colossal material wealth. You must learn to dispose of it as capable and far-sighted masters. With the scope of production which we now have, even fractions of one per cent of spoiled goods in production, or of unnecessary waste, produce great losses. The Leninist motto of economizing, which was especially stressed in the letter of the Central Committee of our Party, the Government, the AUCCTU and of the YCL Central Committee, has been met with a cordial businesslike response in the broad circles of the young people and was supported by the workers, collective farmers and intelligentsia. But this is not the work of one day. We all still have ever so much to do.

Improvement of production, living conditions, and of conditions for rest; intolerance of shortcomings, of all backwardness and manifestations of red-tape—here is where both enthusiasm and a healthy critical attitude, inherent in young people and which needs to be supported, must find their application. It is important to value in the young people the ability to cope with enthusiasm with an assigned task, the ability to react to shortcomings and to overcome them. It is necessary to aspire for the creation of such a spiritual climate in production and in life, in every collective which would elevate man, bring out all of his best abilities and give birth to an irreconcilable attitude towards anti-social acts.

Comrades, communist upbringing of young people was and still is the most important content in the activities of YCL organizations. Young men and women spend in the Komsomol those years of their life when a person's character is moulded, his world outlook is evolved and his stand in life is outlined. If you had not learned at the time how to work diligently and not acquired a taste for knowledge and if you cannot distinguish between truth and falsehood, between the real values of life and the false ones, it will be difficult for you to acquire all that later.

We, Communists, feel happy when we see the improved standards of Marxist-Leninist education of young people and their profound interest in independent study of the works of Vladimir Ilyich Lenin. A study of revolutionary theory requires much and strenuous effort, it is a noble task which enriches man, elevates him to understanding the great tasks of communist construction and makes him a conscious participant in the world revolutionary process. Spare no effort in this work. It is essential, as Engels said, that one should always . . . bear in mind that ever since socialism had become a science, it requires to be treated also as a science, it requires study.

However, young men and women must, if they are to become conscious fighters for the communist cause, absorb, besides theoretical knowledge, also the entire wealth of practical experience, accumulated by the older generations. The Komsomol is called upon to preserve the revolutionary, combat and labour traditions of socialist society, to enrich and multiply them incessantly, not to rest content with the old experiences, but always to move forward.

Our young people must know how to wage an offensive battle against bourgeois ideology. Every YCLer is an active fighter on the ideological front, irreconcilable to all forms of bourgeois influence. There is no place for neutralism and compromise in the struggle between the bourgeois and socialist ideas. We hold sacred Lenin's behest that there can be no concessions on matters "of theory, programme or banner."

Soviet young people are growing up morally healthy, active and purposeful. They are full of energy and enthusiasm in the struggle for the cause of the Party, for the cause of communism. They are young people of a new formation, who have grown up in conditions when socialism has conquered world positions and is ever more determining the trend in world development. The Party has every reason to be proud of Soviet young people, to take pride in the Leninist Komsomol!

Comrades, internationalism has become the flesh and blood of Soviet young people, along with the October Revolution. The heroic achievements of the young generations of the country of the Soviets are the incarnation not only of their limitless love for their Motherland, but also of the high feeling of responsibility for the cause of the international working class, for the ideals of freedom and social justice all over the world.

Our young people are connected by relations of genuine fraternity with young people of the other socialist countries. The people who are now building and fighting within the ranks of the Communist Youth Leagues, and who will tomorrow join the ranks of the ruling Marxist-Leninist Parties, will take upon themselves the noble mission of the consolidation of the world socialist system, and the further raising of its importance in the entire development of the world. There is no doubt that the future of world socialism is in reliable hands.

We are witnesses of the stormy upsurge of the youth movement in capitalist countries. This is an important sign of the aggravation of the general crisis of capitalism. The young people no longer want to reconcile themselves to the system of exploitation and to the sanguinary ventures of imperialism. The mighty demonstrations, staged by the young workers, peasants and students, the mass scale and the militant spirit of their activities has developed in recent years into a serious factor of political struggle in the capitalist countries.

Our Komsomol is paying great attention to the development of friendly ties with the Communist Leagues and other democratic organizations of young people abroad. It takes an active part in all the initiatives and affairs of the World Federation of Democratic Youth and the International Union of Students.

The Party is convinced that the Leninist Komsomol will continue to strengthen the international unity of all the young fighters against imperialism, for peace, freedom and the socialist future of nations.

We live in an age of acute struggle between two social systems in the world arena. Imperialism has not laid down its arms. The international situation makes it obligatory for us to strengthen our defence potential and the combat readiness of the Soviet Armed Forces. This is our sacred duty.

The Army, Navy and Air Force are in need today of people who are educated, ideologically steeled, physically well developed and capable of coupling the traditions of the selfless courage of their fathers with perfect mastery of the newest military equipment. The Komsomol, its glorious detachment in the Army, is of tremendous importance in the nurturing of such reinforcements for the Soviet Armed Forces. This is one of the main areas for the patriotic activities of our Komsomol.

Comrades, all the great labour and combat achievements of our young people were accomplished under the leadership of the Party, which has at its disposal Lenin's arsenal of ways and methods of Party leadership tested by time. The great Lenin taught Communists to be able to lead "by virtue of authority, energy, greater experience, greater versatility, and greater talent."

A businesslike manner, constructive criticism, and adherence to principles, combined with a conscious and, because of that, firm discipline, such are precisely the features of Lenin's style which are characteristic of the life and activities of our Party. Our Komsomol also learns that from the Party. The strength of Soviet young people lies in their inseparable ties with the cause of the Party.

The Central Committee of the Party is convinced that your Congress will evoke the further heightening of initiative on the part of the YCL organizations, and will mobilize the young people of the country to new and glorious deeds. There is no doubt that the Leninist Komsomol will rally its ranks even closer round the Party, and will be even more assiduous in bringing up the young generation in a spirit of infinite loyalty to the people, to the ideals of communism.

We are convinced that the YCLers will be at all times and in every way capable of undertaking the tasks placed before them by the Party, and will continue to be its loyal bulwark in the struggle for communism.

# Part III

FROM THE REPORT TO THE 24TH CPSU CONGRESS

# I

# THE INTERNATIONAL POSITION
# OF THE USSR. THE CPSU'S FOREIGN
# POLICY ACTIVITY

Comrades, our internal development is closely connected with the situation in the world arena. In view of this the Party's Central Committee has devoted much attention to international problems. Plenary Meetings of the CC have repeatedly considered the most important and pressing problems of the USSR's foreign policy, and the CPSU's activity in the communist movement.

The Soviet Union is a peace-loving state, and this is determined by the very nature of our socialist system. The goals of Soviet foreign policy, as formulated by the 23rd Congress of the CPSU, consist in ensuring, together with other socialist countries, favourable international conditions for the construction of socialism and communism; in consolidating the unity and cohesion of the socialist countries, their friendship and brotherhood; supporting the national liberation movement and engaging in all-round co-operation with the young developing states; consistently standing up for the principle of peaceful coexistence between states with different social systems, giving a resolute rebuff to the aggressive forces of imperialism, and safeguarding mankind from another world war.

The whole of the CC's practical activity in the sphere of foreign policy has been designed to achieve these goals.

## 1. For the Further Development of the Friendship and Co-operation of the Socialist Countries

The CC's attention has been constantly centred on questions of further cohesion and development of the world socialist system, and relations with the fraternal socialist countries and their Communist Parties.

The world socialist system has a quarter-century behind it. From the standpoint of development of revolutionary theory and practice these have been exceptionally fruitful years. The socialist world has given the communist and working-class movement experience which is of tremendous and truly historic importance. This experience shows:

• The socialist social system, which is firmly established in the states now constituting the world socialist system, has proved its great viability in the historical contest with capitalism.

• The formation and strengthening of the world socialist system has been a powerful accelerator of historical progress which was started by the Great October Revolution. Fresh prospects have been opened for the triumph of socialism all over the world; life has provided confirmation of the conclusion drawn by the 1969 International Meeting of Communist and Workers' Parties that "the world socialist system is the decisive force in the anti-imperialist struggle."

• The world socialist system has been making a great contribution to the fulfilment of a task of such vital importance for all the peoples as the prevention of another world war. It is safe to say that many of the imperialist aggressors' plans were frustrated thanks to the existence of the world socialist system and its firm action.

• Successes in socialist construction largely depend on the correct combination of the general and the nationally specific in social development. Not only are we now theoretically aware but also have been convinced in practice that the way to socialism and its main features are determined by the general regularities, which are inherent in the development of all the socialist countries. We are also aware that the effect of the general regularities is manifested in different forms consistent with concrete historical conditions and national specifics. It is impossible to build socialism without basing oneself on general regularities or taking account of the concrete historical specifics of each country. Nor is it possible without a consideration of both these factors correctly to develop relations between the socialist states.

The experience accumulated over the quarter-century also makes it possible to take a more profound and more realistic approach in assessing and determining the ways of overcoming objective and subjective difficulties which arise in the construction of the new society and the establishment of the new, socialist type of inter-state relations. Given a correct policy of the Marxist-Leninist Parties, the common social system, and the identity of basic interests and purposes of the peoples of the socialist countries make it possible successfully to overcome these difficulties and steadily to advance the cause of developing and strengthening the world socialist system.

The past five-year period has seen a considerable contribution to the treasure-house of the collective experience of the fraternal countries and Parties. In the last five years, the economic potential of the socialist states has increased substantially, the political foundations of socialism have been strengthened, the people's living standards have been raised, and culture and science have been further developed.

At the same time, it is known that some difficulties and complications have continued to appear in the socialist world, and this has also had an effect on the development of relations between individual states and the Soviet Union. However, this has not changed the dominant tendency of strengthening friendship and cohesion of the socialist countries. On the whole, our co-operation with the fraternal countries has been successfully developing and strengthening in every sphere.

The CPSU has attached special importance to developing *co-operation with the Communist Parties of the fraternal countries*. This co-operation, enriching us with each other's experience, has enabled us jointly to work on the fundamental problems of socialist and communist construction, to find the most rational forms of economic relations, collectively to lay down a common line in foreign affairs, and to exchange opinion on questions relating to the work in the sphere of ideology and culture.

The period under review was marked by important successes in *co-ordinating the foreign-policy activity* of the fraternal Parties and states. The most important international problems and events in this period were considered collectively by the representatives of socialist countries on various levels.

The Warsaw Treaty Organisation has been and continues to be the main centre for co-ordinating the foreign-policy activity of the fraternal countries.

The Warsaw Treaty countries displayed the initiative of putting forward a full-scale programme for strengthening peace in Europe, which is pivoted on the demand that the immutability of the existing state borders should be secured. The Political Consultative Committee has devoted several of its sittings to formulating and concretising this programme.

The Warsaw Treaty countries can also undoubtedly count among their political assets the fact that the plans which had existed within NATO to give the FRG militarists access to nuclear weapons have not been realised.

Joint efforts by the socialist states have also made it possible to achieve substantial progress in solving a task of such importance for stabilising the situation in Europe as the strengthening of the international positions of the German Democratic Republic. The so-called Hallstein Doctrine has been defeated. The GDR has already been recognised by 27 states, and this process is bound to continue.

Active and consistent support from the Soviet Union and other socialist countries is vitally important for the struggle of the peoples of Vietnam and the other countries of Indochina against the imperialist interventionists. The steps taken by the socialist states in the Middle East have become one of the decisive factors which have frustrated the imperialist plans of overthrowing the progressive regimes in the Arab countries.

In the United Nations and other international bodies, the socialist countries, acting together, have put forward many proposals of key international importance. These proposals have been at the focus of world opinion.

As a result of the collective formulation and implementation of a number of measures in recent years, the *military organisation of the Warsaw Treaty* has been further improved. The armed forces of the allied powers are in a state of high readiness and are capable of guaranteeing the peaceful endeavour of the fraternal peoples.

In short, comrades, the socialist countries' multilateral political co-operation is becoming ever closer and more vigorous. We set ourselves definite aims and work jointly to achieve them. This is naturally of tremendous importance, especially in the present conditions of the contest between the two world social systems.

Of equal importance is *co-operation in the economic sphere,* and extension and deepening of national-economic ties between the socialist countries. The period under review has also been fruitful in this respect.

Let us turn to the facts.

The Soviet Union and the fraternal states seek to help each other in every way to develop their national economies. In the last five years, over 300 industrial and agricultural projects have been built or reconstructed in the socialist countries with our technical assistance. We have been supplying our friends with many types of industrial products on mutually advantageous terms. The Soviet Union has met 70, and more, per cent of the import requirements in some key types of raw materials and fuel of the CMEA countries and Cuba, and also to a considerable extent those of the Democratic Republic of Vietnam and the Korean People's Democratic Republic.

In the past five-year period, our national economy, for its part, has received from the CMEA countries equipment for 54 chemical plants. Over 38 per cent of the seagoing tonnage which our merchant navy has received in that period was made at our friends' shipyards. The CMEA countries are taking part through their investments in developing raw material and fuel branches of the Soviet economy, and in enlarging the capacities for making metal, mineral fertilisers and pulp. We have also been receiving many consumer goods from the fraternal countries.

The USSR and the other CMEA countries arrange their economic relations on a long-term basis. In particular, the fraternal countries have co-ordinated their national-economic plans for 1971–1975. In the last few years, active work has been continued in developing the organisational structure and technical basis for multilateral economic co-operation.

The second section of the Druzhba oil pipeline is being laid. In the first year of its operation, 1964, it carried 8.3 million tons of oil, and in 1975 the fraternal countries will receive almost 50 million tons of oil. A gas pipeline of unique dimensions is being laid to carry natural gas from Siberia to the country's European part. This will also help to increase gas deliveries to Czechoslovakia and Poland, and to start supplying gas to the GDR, Bulgaria and Hungary. The Mir integrated power grids have been yielding great economies for the CMEA countries. The International Bank for Economic Co-operation has been operating successfully, and a common investment bank of the CMEA countries recently started operations. Other forms of multilateral ties are also being strengthened.

All this has produced its results, helping to make social production more efficient, and to develop the national economy of each of our countries at a rapid pace. In the past five-year period, the CMEA countries' industrial production increased by 49 per cent. Trade between them has also been growing.

However, like other members of CMEA, we believe that the possibilities of the socialist division of labour are not yet being fully used. Practice has led us up to this common conclusion: it is necessary to deepen specialisation and co-operation of production, and to tie in our national-economic plans more closely, that is, to advance along the way of the socialist countries' economic integration. Comrades, this is an important and necessary endeavour.

The economic integration of the socialist countries is a new and complex process. It implies a new and broader approach to many economic questions, and the ability to find the most rational solutions, meeting the interests not only of the given country but of all the participants in co-operation. It requires firm orientation on the latest scientific and technical achievements, and the most profitable and technically advanced lines of production.

That is the approach the CPSU intends to foster among workers in our planning and economic bodies. In this connection consideration should also apparently be given to the steps that would provide every unit of our economic system with an incentive to develop long-term economic ties with the fraternal countries.

In the period between the 23rd and the 24th Congresses, our Party has displayed much concern for strengthening *bilateral relations between the Soviet Union* and the socialist countries.

Close and diverse co-operation, friendship and cordiality are characteristic of our relations with the Warsaw Treaty countries—Bulgaria, Hungary, the German Democratic Republic, Poland, Rumania and Czechoslovakia.

New treaties of friendship, co-operation and mutual assistance have been concluded with Bulgaria, Hungary, Czechoslovakia and Rumania. Together with the treaties with the GDR, Poland and Mongolia, which entered into force earlier, together with the other bilateral treaties between the fraternal countries, these documents constitute a comprehensive system of mutual allied commitments of a new, socialist type.

Our friendship with the Polish People's Republic is unshakeable. We note with deep satisfaction that the difficulties which arose in fraternal Poland have been overcome. The Polish United Workers' Party is taking steps to have its ties with the working class and all other working people strengthened, and the positions of socialism in the country consolidated. From the bottom of their hearts, the Communists of the Soviet Union wish their Polish friends the very greatest of success.

Our Party, and the Soviet people have relations of socialist solidarity and strong and militant friendship with the Working People's Party of Vietnam and the Democratic Republic of Vietnam. Following the precepts of Ho Chi Minh, great patriot and revolutionary, the Vietnamese people have raised high the banner of socialism and are fearlessly confronting the imperialist aggressors. The Democratic Republic of Vietnam may be sure that in its armed struggle and its peaceful endeavour it can continue to rely on the Soviet Union's fraternal support.

Over these years, the Central Committee has devoted constant attention to strengthening co-operation with the Republic of Cuba and the Communist Party of Cuba. As a result of joint efforts, considerable successes have been achieved in developing Soviet-Cuban relations. The peoples of the Soviet Union and of Cuba are comrades-in-arms in a common struggle, and their friendship is firm.

For half a century now, the CPSU and the Soviet state have had bonds of strong and time-tested friendship with the Mongolian People's Revolutionary Party and the Mongolian People's Republic. The Soviet Union is a true friend and ally of socialist Mongolia, and actively supports the efforts of our Mongolian friends aimed at solving major economic problems and strengthening their country's international positions.

In the last few years, our ties with the Korean People's Democratic Republic and the Korean Party of Labour have grown, and this, we are sure, meets the interests of the peoples of both countries. The Soviet Union has supported and continues to support the proposals of the KPDR Government on the country's peaceful, democratic unification, and the Korean people's demands for a withdrawal of US troops from the south of Korea.

In the period under review, Soviet-Yugoslav relations have continued to develop. The Soviet people want to see socialism in Yugoslavia strengthened, and her ties with the socialist community growing stronger. We stand for Soviet-Yugoslav co-operation, and for developing contacts between our Parties.

About our relations with the People's Republic of China. It will be recalled that the Chinese leaders have put forward an ideological-political platform of their own which is incompatible with Leninism on the key questions of international life and the world communist movement, and have demanded that we should abandon the line of the 20th Congress and the Programme of the CPSU. They unfolded an intensive and hostile propaganda campaign against our Party and country, made territorial claims on the Soviet Union, and in the spring and summer of 1969 brought things to the point of armed incidents along the border.

Our Party has resolutely opposed the attempts to distort the Marxist-Leninist teaching, and to split the international communist movement and the ranks of the fighters against imperialism. Displaying restraint and refusing to be provoked, the CC CPSU and the Soviet Government have done their utmost to bring about a normalisation of relations with the People's Republic of China.

In the last eighteen months, as a result of the initiative displayed on our part, there have been signs of some normalisation in relations between the USSR and the PRC. A meeting of the heads of government of the two countries took place in September 1969, and this was followed by negotiations in Peking between government delegations on a settlement of the border issues. These negotiations are proceeding slowly, and it goes without saying that their favourable completion calls for a constructive attitude not only of one side.

An exchange of ambassadors took place between the USSR and the PRC at the end of last year. After a considerable interval, trade agreements have been signed and trade has somewhat increased. These are useful steps. We are prepared to continue to act in this direction.

But on the other hand, comrades, we cannot, of course, fail to see that the anti-Soviet line in China's propaganda and policy is being continued, and that the 9th Congress of the CPC has written this line, which is hostile to the Soviet Union, into its decisions.

What can be said in this context?

We resolutely reject the slanderous inventions concerning the policy of our Party and our state which are being spread from Peking and instilled into the minds of the Chinese people. It is the more absurd and harmful to sow dissent between China and the USSR considering that this is taking place in a situation in which the imperialists have been stepping up their aggressive action against the freedom-loving peoples. More than ever before the situation demands cohesion and joint action by all the anti-imperialist, revolutionary forces, instead of fanning hostility between such states as the USSR and China.

We shall never forsake the national interests of the Soviet state. The CPSU will continue tirelessly to work for the cohesion of the socialist countries and the world communist movement on a Marxist-Leninist basis. At the same time, our Party and the Soviet Government are deeply convinced that an improvement of relations between the Soviet Union and the People's Republic of China would be in line with the fundamental, long-term interests of both countries, the interests of socialism, the freedom of the peoples, and stronger peace. That is why we are prepared in every way to help not only to normalise relations but also to restore neighbourliness and friendship between the Soviet Union and the People's Republic of China and express the confidence that this will eventually be achieved.

Such is our principled stand. We have repeatedly stated it, are firmly committed to it, and are backing it up in practice.

As regards Albania, we are prepared, as in the past, to restore normal relations with her. This would be beneficial to both countries and to the common interests of the socialist states.

Comrades, the political crisis in Czechoslovakia has been fairly prominent in the international events of recent years.

There is apparently no need here to set out the factual side of the matter, which is well known. Let us deal only with some of the conclusions drawn from what has taken place which we believe to be the most essential.

The Czechoslovak events were a fresh reminder that in the countries which have taken the path of socialist construction the internal anti-socialist forces, whatever remained of them, may, in certain conditions, become active and even mount direct counter-revolutionary action in the hope of support from outside, from imperialism, which, for its part, is always prepared to form blocs with such forces.

The danger of Right-wing revisionism, which seeks, on the pretext of "improving" socialism, to destroy the revolutionary essence of Marxism-Leninism, and paves the way for the penetration of bourgeois ideology, has been fully brought out in this connection.

The Czechoslovak events showed very well how important it is constantly to strengthen the Party's leading role in socialist society, steadily to improve the forms and methods of Party leadership, and to display a creative Marxist-Leninist approach to the solution of pressing problems of socialist development.

It was quite clear to us that this was not only an attempt on the part of imperialism and its accomplices to overthrow the socialist system in Czechoslovakia. It was an attempt to strike in this way at the positions of socialism in Europe as a whole, and to create favourable conditions for a subsequent onslaught against the socialist world by the most aggressive forces of imperialism.

In view of the appeals by Party and state leaders, Communists and working people of Czechoslovakia, and considering the danger posed to the socialist gains in that country, we and the fraternal socialist countries then jointly took a decision to render internationalist assistance to Czechoslovakia in defence of socialism. In the extraordinary conditions created by the forces of imperialism and counter-revolution, we were bound to do so by our class duty, loyalty to socialist internationalism, and the concern for the interests of our states and the future of socialism and peace in Europe.

You will recall that in its document, "Lessons of the Crisis Development," a plenary meeting of the CC of the Communist Party of Czechoslovakia gave this assessment of the importance of the fraternal states' collective assistance (I quote):

"The entry of the allied troops of the five socialist countries into Czechoslovakia was an act of international solidarity, meeting both the common interests of the Czechoslovakian working people and the interests of the international working class, the socialist community and the class interests of the international communist movement. This internationalist act saved the lives of thousands of men, ensured internal and external conditions for peaceful and tranquil labour, strengthened the Western borders of the socialist camp, and blasted the hopes of the imperialist circles for a revision of the results of the Second World War."

We fully agree with the conclusion drawn by the Communist Party of Czechoslovakia. Life has once again provided convincing evidence that the fraternal unity of the socialist countries is the most reliable barrier against the forces trying to attack, and weaken, the socialist camp, to undermine and invalidate the working people's socialist gains. The peoples of the socialist countries have clearly demonstrated to the whole world that they will not give up their revolutionary gains, and that the borders of the socialist community are immutable and inviolable.

We are sincerely glad that the Communists of Czechoslovakia have successfully stood the trials that fell to their lot. Today the Communist Party of Czechoslovakia is advancing towards its 14th Congress, which we are sure will be a new and important stage in strengthening the positions of socialism in Czechoslovakia.

Comrades, the present-day socialist world, with its successes and prospects, with all its problems, is still a young and growing social organism, where not everything has settled and where much still bears the marks of earlier historical epochs.

The socialist world is forging ahead and is continuously improving. Its development naturally runs through struggle between the new and the old, through the resolution of internal contradictions. The experience that has been accumulated helps the fraternal Parties to find correct and timely resolution of the contradictions and confidently to advance along the path indicated by Marx, Engels and Lenin, the great teachers of the proletariat.

The Communist Party of the Soviet Union has regarded and continues to regard as its internationalist duty in every way to promote the further growth of the might of the world socialist system. Our stand is that the co-operation between the fraternal countries should grow ever more diverse and gain in depth, that it should involve ever broader masses of working people, and that each other's concrete experience should be more fundamentally studied at every level of state, social, economic and cultural life.

We want to see every fraternal country a flourishing state, harmoniously combining rapid economic, scientific and technical growth with a flowering of socialist culture and rising living standards for the working people. We want the world socialist system to be a well-knit family of nations, building and defending the new society together, and mutually enriching each other with experience and knowledge, a family, strong and united, which the people of the world would regard as the prototype of the future world community of free nations.

Allow me to assure our friends, our brothers and our comrades-in-arms in the socialist countries that the Communist Party of the Soviet Union will spare no effort to attain this lofty goal!

## 2. Imperialism, Enemy of the Peoples and Social Progress. The Peoples Against Imperialism

Comrades, at its 23rd Congress and then in a number of its documents our Party has already given a comprehensive assessment of modern imperialism. A Marxist-Leninist analysis of its present-day features is contained in the material of the 1969 International Communist Meeting. Allow me, therefore, in the light of the experience of the last few years to deal only with some of the basic points which we must take account of in our policy.

The features of contemporary capitalism largely spring from the fact that it is trying to adapt itself to the new situation in the world. In the conditions of the confrontation with socialism, the ruling circles of the capitalist countries are afraid more than they have ever been of the class struggle developing into a massive revolutionary movement. Hence, the bourgeoisie's striving to use more camouflaged forms of exploitation and oppression of the working people, and its readiness now and again to agree to partial reforms in order to keep the masses under its ideological and political control as far as possible. The monopolies have been making extensive use of scientific and technical achievements to fortify their positions, to enhance the efficiency and accelerate the pace of production, and to intensify the exploitation and oppression of the working people.

However, adaptation to the new conditions does not mean that capitalism has been stabilised as a system. *The general crisis of capitalism has continued to deepen.*

Even the most developed capitalist states are not free from grave economic upheavals. The USA, for instance, has been floundering in one of its economic crises for almost two years now. The last few years have also been marked by a grave crisis in the capitalist monetary and financial system. The simultaneous growth of inflation and unemployment has become a permanent feature. There are now almost eight million unemployed in the developed capitalist countries.

The contradictions between the imperialist states have not been eliminated either by the processes of integration or the imperialists' class concern for pooling their efforts in fighting against the socialist world. By the early 1970s, the main centres of imperialist rivalry have become clearly visible: these are the USA—Western Europe (above all, the six Common Market countries)—Japan. The economic and political competitive struggle between them has been growing ever more acute. The import bans imposed by official US agencies on an ever growing number of products from Europe and Japan, and the European countries' efforts to limit their exploitation by US capital are only some of the signs of this struggle.

In the past five-year period, imperialist foreign policy has provided fresh evidence that imperialism has not ceased to be reactionary and aggressive.

In this context, one must deal above all with US imperialism, which in the last few years has reasserted its urge to act as a kind of guarantor and protector of the international system of exploitation and oppression. It seeks to dominate everywhere, interferes in the affairs of other peoples, high-handedly tramples on their legitimate rights and sovereignty, and seeks by force, bribery and economic penetration to impose its will on states and whole areas of the world.

Needless to say, the forces of war and aggression also exist in the other imperialist countries. In West Germany, these are the revanchists, who have been increasingly ganging up with the neo-Nazis; in Britain, these are the executioners of Northern Ireland, the suppliers of arms to the South African racists, and the advocates of the aggressive US policy; in Japan, these are the militarists who, in defiance of the constitution, which prohibits war "for all time," seek once again to push the country onto the path of expansion and aggression.

Another fact, comrades, that should also be borne in mind is that since the war militarism in the capitalist world has been growing on an unprecedented scale. This tendency has been intensified in the recent period. In 1970 alone, the NATO countries invested 103 thousand million dollars in war preparations. Militarisation has acquired the most dangerous nature in the USA. In the last five years, that country has spent almost 400 thousand million dollars for military purposes.

The imperialists have been systematically plundering the peoples of dozens of countries in Asia, Africa, and Latin Amer-

ica. Every year, they funnel thousands of millions of dollars
out of the Third World. Meanwhile, according to a 1970 UN
report on the world food situation, 375 million people on
these continents live on the brink of death from starvation.

The imperialists are prepared to commit any crime in their
efforts to preserve or restore their domination of the peoples in
their former colonies or in other countries which are escaping
from the grip of capitalist exploitation. The last five-year period has provided much fresh evidence of this. The aggression
against the Arab states, the colonialist attempts to invade
Guinea, and the subversive activity against the progressive regimes in Latin America—all this is a constant reminder that the
imperialist war against the freedom-loving peoples has not
ceased.

And the continuing US aggression against the peoples of
Vietnam, Cambodia and Laos is the main atrocity committed
by the modern colonialists; it is the stamp of ignominy of the
United States.

In the last few years, facts about the war crimes of US imperialism have come to light that have literally rocked world public opinion. Tragic notoriety fell to the lot of the Vietnamese
village of Song My, whose unarmed civilian population, including old men, women and children, was sadistically wiped
out by the US executioners.

It is hard to keep a calm tone when speaking about the
atrocities committed by the interventionists, who are armed to
the teeth. Hundreds of thousands of tons of napalm have literally scorched into wasteland whole areas of South Vietnam. Almost 1.5 million Vietnamese have been poisoned, and many
have died as a result of the use of chemical weapons. No honest man, least of all a Communist, can ever reconcile his conscience with what is being done by the US interventionists and
their henchmen, who claim to represent "Western civilisation"
and the so-called "free world." It is a disgrace!

Comrades, we have no doubt at all that the attempts of imperialism to turn the tide of history, to make it flow in its favour, are bound to fail. However, we Communists are well

aware that there is no room for passivity or self-complacency. The fighters against capitalist oppression are confronted by the last but the most powerful of the exploiting systems that have ever existed. That is why a long and hard struggle still lies ahead.

But however hard this struggle, it continues to mount and its front is being steadily widened. In the last few years, the fighters against imperialism have written new and glorious pages into the annals of the class battles.

The *international working-class movement* continues to play, as it has played in the past, the role of time-tested and militant vanguard of the revolutionary forces. The events of the past five-year period in the capitalist world have fully borne out the importance of the working class as the chief and strongest opponent of the rule of the monopolies, and as a centre rallying all the anti-monopoly forces.

In countries like France and Italy, where the traditions of the class struggle are more developed, and where strong Communist Parties are active, the working people, headed by the working class, have attacked not only individual groups of capitalists, but the whole system of state-monopoly domination. In Britain, the class struggle has reached a high state of tension, and the current strikes are comparable in scale and in the numbers involved only with the general strike of 1926. In the USA, working-class action against the monopolies has assumed great scope, and the struggle of the Negro people for equality, and of youth against the war in Vietnam is spreading with unprecedented acerbity. The mass working-class movement in the FRG is gathering momentum. For the first time in many decades, large-scale class clashes have taken place in the Scandinavian countries and in Holland. The socio-political crisis in Spain continues to sharpen. In all the class battles of the recent period, the working people's trade unions, especially those brought together within the World Federation of Trade Unions, have played a considerable and increasingly important role.

The Meeting of the fraternal Parties, it will be recalled, drew the conclusion that the current large-scale battles of the working class are a harbinger of fresh class battles which could lead to fundamental social change, to the establishment of the power of the working class in alliance with other sections of the working people.

At the same time, comrades, imperialism is being subjected to ever greater pressure by the forces which have sprung from the national liberation struggle, above all by the young independent and anti-imperialist-minded states of Asia and Africa.

The main thing is that *the struggle for national liberation in many countries has in practical terms begun to grow into a struggle against exploitative relations, both feudal and capitalist.*

Today, there are already quite a few countries in Asia and Africa which have taken the non-capitalist way of development, that is, the path of building a socialist society in the long term. Many states have now taken this path. Deep-going social changes, which are in the interests of the masses of people, and which lead to a strengthening of national independence, are being implemented in these countries, and the number of these changes has been growing as time goes on.

The offensive by the forces of national and social liberation against domination by imperialism is expressed in various forms. Thus, in the countries oriented towards socialism the property of the imperialist monopolies is being nationalised. This makes it possible to strengthen and develop the state sector, which is essentially an economic basis for a revolutionary-democratic policy. In a country like the United Arab Republic, the state sector now accounts for 85 per cent of total industrial production, and in Burma, the state sector controls over 80 per cent of the extractive and almost 60 per cent of the manufacturing industry. New serious steps in nationalising imperialist property have been taken in Algeria. Many foreign enterprises, banks and trading companies have been handed over to the state in Guinea, the Sudan, Somali and Tanzania.

Serious steps have also been taken to solve the land problem, which is complicated and has a bearing on the lot of many millions of peasants. Taking the past five-year period alone, important agrarian transformations have been carried out in the UAR and Syria, and have been started in the Sudan and Somali. An agrarian reform has been announced for this year in Algeria. In the People's Republic of the Congo (Brazzaville), all the land and its minerals have been handed over into the ownership of the state.

Needless to say, it is no easy thing to bring about a radical restructuring of backward social relations on non-capitalist principles, and in an atmosphere of unceasing attacks by the neocolonialists and domestic reactionaries. This makes it all the more important that despite all these difficulties the states taking the socialist orientation have been further advancing along their chosen path.

Progressive social change has not advanced to that point in all the former colonies and dependent countries. But the struggle against the forces of reaction and against the henchmen of imperialism is being carried on everywhere, and in some countries the progressive forces have already scored serious gains. One need merely recall, for instance, events like the recent nationalisation of the big banks in India, and the impressive victory scored over the Right-wing forces at the last elections to the House of the People of the Indian Parliament. This is evidence that the masses of people in that country resolutely oppose the reactionary pro-imperialist forces, and stand for the implementation of a land reform and other socio-economic transformations, and for a policy of peace and friendship in international affairs. Considerable social shifts have taken place in Ceylon and Nigeria.

Despite all the difficulties and even occasional defeats, a diversified process of social change is going on in vast areas of the world. The working people have been scoring important victories in the fight for their rights, for real freedom and for human dignity. The patriots of countries still burdened by the colonial yoke are continuing their courageous fight for liberation.

As to our country, it fully supports this just struggle. The

USSR's political and economic co-operation with the liberated countries has been further developed in the last few years. Our trade with them is growing. Dozens of industrial and agricultural enterprises have been built in many countries of Asia and Africa with our participation. We have also been making a contribution to the training of personnel for these countries. All this is being done in the mutual interest.

Great changes have been taking place in a number of Latin American countries. The victory of the Popular Unity Forces in Chile was a most important event. There, for the first time in the history of the continent, the people have secured, by constitutional means, the installation of a government they want and trust. This has incensed domestic reaction and Yankee imperialism, which seek to deprive the Chilean people of their gains. However the people of Chile are fully determined to advance along their chosen path. The working people of other Latin American countries have come out in support of Chile's progressive line. The governments of Peru and Bolivia are fighting against enslavement by the US monopolies.

The great Lenin's prediction that the peoples of the colonies and dependent countries, starting with a struggle for national liberation, would go on to a fight against the very foundations of the exploitative system is coming true. And this means, of course, a most heavy blow at the positions of capitalism as a whole, as a world social system.

Comrades, success in the struggle against imperialism largely depends on the cohesion of the anti-imperialist forces, above all of *the world communist movement*, their vanguard. In the last five years, our Party together with the other fraternal Parites, has done much to strengthen this cohesion and the unity of the communist ranks.

It was a complex task. It was precisely in the period under review that the attempts on various sides to attack Marxism-Leninism as the ideological-theoretical basis for the activity of the communist movement have been most acute. The Chinese leadership went over to the establishment in a number of countries of splinter groupings under the signboard of the so-called

"Marxist-Leninist parties," and has clearly tried to unite them in some way as a counterweight to the international communist movement. The Trotskyites have now and again formed blocs with these groupings. Here and there tendencies towards nationalistic self-isolation have been stepped up, and both "Left" and Right-wing opportunism have been revived.

The main aim has been to secure a turn towards the cohesion of the communist movement and a consolidation of its ideological basis. An important stage in the efforts to attain it was the 1967 conference of European Communist Parties at Karlovy Vary and also a number of other international meetings of Communists.

As a result the question of calling an International Meeting of Communist and Workers' Parties was placed on the order of the day. It was preceded by much preparatory work. You are aware, comrades, that a considerable contribution to the elaboration of the idea of the Meeting and to its preparation was made by our Party, by the CC CPSU.

The Meeting was a major step forward in strengthening the international unity of the Communists and in consolidating all the anti-imperialist forces. It has done a great deal for developing a number of propositions of Marxist-Leninist theory as applied to the present-day situation. It has been confirmed that this broadest and most representative form of intercourse between the fraternal Parties meets the needs of the communist movement as an international force. Our Party is in complete agreement with the conclusion drawn by the participants in the Meeting about the advisability of holding such international forums of fraternal Parties as the need arises. It would be useful for them to become an established practice of the world communist movement.

The celebrations of the Lenin Centenary, which became truly world-wide, were also of tremendous importance for the cohesion of the communist movement. The Meeting of Communist Parties and the Lenin Centenary once again showed the viability of the Marxist-Leninist teaching and brought about an upswing in the fraternal Parties' activity in the fight for the interests of the working class and all working people, and against imperialism, and its minions in the working-class movement.

On the whole there is ground to say that cohesion in the international communist movement is being increasingly strengthened, and that fruitful bilateral and multilateral inter-Party ties are becoming ever more active. Our Party welcomes this. It will work further to make sure that such development will continue precisely in this direction.

However, comrades, another fact we cannot afford to lose sight of is that negative phenomena have not yet been overcome everywhere. The fight against Right and "Left"-wing revisionism, against nationalism, continues to be urgent. It is precisely the nationalistic tendencies, especially those which assume the form of anti-Sovietism, that bourgeois ideologists and bourgeois propaganda have most willingly relied upon in their fight against socialism and the communist movement. They have been trying to induce the opportunist elements in the Communist Parties to make something of an ideological deal. They appear to be telling them: just give us proof that you are anti-Sovieteers, and then we shall be prepared to proclaim that you are the true "Marxists," and that you are taking completely "independent attitudes." The course of events has shown, incidentally, that such men also take the way of struggle against the Communist Parties in their own countries. Examples of this are renegades of the type of Garaudy in France, Fischer in Austria, Petkov in Venezuela, and the "Manifesto" group leaders in Italy. The fraternal Parties regard the fight against such elements as an important condition for strengthening their ranks. Consequently, even these examples—and their number could be easily multiplied—testify that the struggle against revisionism and nationalism continues to be an important task of the Communist Parties.

Comrades, in the struggle against imperialism an ever greater role is being played by the revolutionary-democratic parties, many of which have proclaimed socialism as their programme goal. The CPSU has been actively developing its ties with them. We are sure that co-operation between such parties and the Communist Parties, including those in their own countries, fully meets the interests of the anti-imperialist movement, the strengthening of national independence and the cause of social progress.

We maintain and have been developing relations with the Left Socialist parties in some countries of the West, East and Latin America. Fairly active work has been carried on on this plane in the last few years.

In accordance with the line laid down by the 1969 International Meeting, the CPSU is prepared to develop co-operation with the Social-Democrats both in the struggle for peace and democracy, and in the struggle for socialism, without, of course, making any concessions in ideology and revolutionary principles. However, this line of the Communists has been meeting with stubborn resistance from the Right-wing leaders of the Social-Democrats. Our Party has carried on and will continue to carry on an implacable struggle against any attitudes which tend to subordinate the working-class movement to the interests of monopoly capital, and to undermine the cause of the working people's struggle for peace, democracy and socialism.

Comrades, to the lot of the Communists have fallen the hardest trials of any that have ever fallen to the lot of fighters for the people's cause. We remember these words of Lenin's: "Selfless devotion to the revolution and revolutionary propaganda among the people are not wasted even if long decades divide the sowing from the harvest." The ideas of the Communists have sprouted remarkable shoots in the practice of real socialism, and in the thoughts and deeds of millions upon millions of men.

The Communists of the Soviet Union put a high value on the tremendous work which is being done in their countries by the fraternal Communist and Workers' Parties. We are well aware how hard this work is, how much selfless dedication and boundless loyalty to our common great ideals it requires. Today we should like once again to assure our comrades-in-arms

—the Communists of the whole world: our Party, dear friends, will always march in closely serried, fighting ranks together with you!

We shall never forget the great sacrifices that have been made in the struggle. The names of the heroes of the communist movement, and the feats of courage and loyalty to the working-class cause will always remain sacred for all true revolutionaries. They will always remain sacred for Lenin's Party, for the Soviet people, which first raised the banner of victorious socialist revolution.

Conscious of its internationalist duty, the Communist Party of the Soviet Union will continue to pursue a line in international affairs which helps further to invigorate the world-wide anti-imperialist struggle, and to strengthen the fighting unity of all its participants.

The full triumph of the socialist cause all over the world is inevitable. And we shall not spare ourselves in the fight for this triumph, for the happiness of the working people!

### 3. The Soviet Union's Struggle for Peace and the Security of Peoples. Rebuff to the Imperialist Policy of Aggression

Comrades, in the period under review the Central Committee and the Soviet Government did their utmost to ensure peaceful conditions for communist construction in the USSR, to expose and frustrate action by the aggressive imperialist forces, and to defend socialism, the freedom of peoples and peace.

Our policy has always combined firm rebuffs to aggression, and the constructive line of settling pressing international problems, and maintaining normal, and, wherever the situation allows, good, relations with states belonging to the other social system. As in the past, we have consistently stood up for the Leninist principle of peaceful coexistence of states, regardless of their social system. This principle has now become a real force of international development.

Let me deal with the most important international problems which because of their acerbity or importance for the future have required our special attention.

To start with the events in South-East Asia. The aggressive war started by US ruling circles in that part of the world has not brought the American people any victorious laurels but tens of thousands of funeral wreaths. Anyone capable of taking a realistic view of things must realise that neither direct armed intervention, nor torpedoing of negotiations, nor even the ever wider use of mercenaries will break down the Vietnamese people's determination to become master of its own country.

The so-called Vietnamisation of the war, that is, the plan to have Vietnamese kill Vietnamese in Washington's interests, and the extension of the aggression to Cambodia and Laos—none of this will get the USA out of the bog of its dirty war in Indochina or wash away the shame heaped on that country by those who started and are continuing the aggression. There is only one way of solving the Vietnamese problem. It is clearly indicated in the proposals of the DRV Government and the Provisional Revolutionary Government of the Republic of South Vietnam, proposals which we firmly back.

The Soviet Union resolutely demands an end to the imperialist aggression against the peoples of Vietnam, Cambodia and Laos. Our country has been and will be an active champion of the just cause of the heroic peoples of Indochina.

The Middle East is another "hot spot" in world politics.

The crisis which has arisen as a result of Israel's attack on the UAR, Syria and Jordan has been one of the most intense in the development of international relations over the past period.

Together with the fraternal socialist countries we did everything necessary to stop and condemn the aggression. We raised this question in the UN Security Council in the most resolute terms. An extraordinary session of the General Assembly was called on our demand. The USSR and other fraternal countries have broken off diplomatic relations with Israel, which has ignored the UN decision for a ceasefire. Our country has helped to restore the defence potential of the Arab states which were subjected to invasion, the UAR and Syria in the first place, with whom our co-operation has been growing stronger from year to year.

The United Arab Republic recently came out with important initiatives. It announced its acceptance of the proposal put forward by the UN special representative, Dr. Gunnar Jarring, and readiness to conclude a peace agreement with Israel once the Israeli troops are withdrawn from the occupied Arab territories. The UAR has also proposed steps to resume navigation along the Suez Canal in the very near future. Thus, the attitude of the Arab side provides a real basis for settling the crisis in the Middle East. The Israeli Government's rejection of all these proposals, and Tel Aviv's now openly brazen claims to Arab lands clearly show who is blocking the way to peace in the Middle East, and who is to blame for the dangerous hotbed of war being maintained in that area. At the same time, the unseemly role of those who are instigating the Israeli extremists, the role of US imperialism and of international Zionism as an instrument of the aggressive imperialist circles, is becoming ever more obvious.

However, Tel Aviv ought to take a sober view of things. Do Israel's ruling circles really expect to secure for themselves the lands of others they have occupied and to go scot-free? In the final count, the advantages obtained by the invaders as a result of their piratical attack are illusory. They will disappear as mirages pass from view in the sands of Sinai. And the longer the delay in reaching a political settlement in the Middle East, the stronger will be the indignation of world public opinion, and the Arab peoples' hatred of the aggressor and its patrons, and the greater the harm the Israeli rulers will inflict on their people and their country.

The Soviet Union will continue its firm support of its Arab friends. Our country is prepared to join other powers, who are permanent members of the Security Council, in providing international guarantees for a political settlement in the Middle East.

Once this is reached, we feel that there could be a consideration of further steps designed for a military détente in the whole area, in particular, for converting the Mediterranean into a sea of peace and friendly co-operation.

Comrades, Europe has been one of the most important lines in our foreign policy activity all these years.

The improvement in Soviet-French relations has had important positive consequences for the whole course of European affairs. As a result of the recent talks in Moscow with the President of France and the signing of a Protocol on Political Consultations, the possibilities of Soviet-French co-operation have been extended. Our peoples' friendship rests on sound historical traditions. Today, our states also have an extensive sphere of common interests. We stand for the further development and deepening of relations between the USSR and France, and regard this as an important factor of international security.

New prospects in Europe are opening up as a result of a substantial shift in our relations with the FRG.

Throughout the whole postwar period, we, like our allies and friends, have proceeded from the fact that lasting peace in Europe rests above all on the inviolability of the borders of European states. Now, the treaties of the Soviet Union and Poland with the FRG have confirmed with full certainty the inviolability of borders, including those between the GDR and the FRG, and the western border of the Polish state.

There is a sharp demarcation of political forces in West Germany over the ratification of these treaties. One would assume that realistic-minded circles in Bonn, and also in some other Western capitals, are aware of this simple truth: delay over ratification would produce a fresh crisis of confidence over the whole of the FRG's policy, and would worsen the political climate in Europe and the prospects for easing international tensions.

As for the Soviet Union, it is prepared to meet the commitments it has assumed under the Soviet-West-German treaty. We are prepared to cover our part of the way towards normalisation and improvement of relations between the FRG and the socialist part of Europe, provided, of course, the other side acts in accordance with the letter and spirit of the treaty.

The positive changes that have recently taken place in Europe do not mean that the problems Europe inherited from the Second World War have been fully solved. What is to be done to continue the improvement in the European situation, to make headway in ensuring collective security in Europe, and in developing co-operation both on a bilateral and on an all-European basis?

An improvement of the situation in Europe as a whole could be served by the convocation of an all-European conference. This is now being backed by a majority of the European states. Preparations for it are being carried into the plane of practical politics. But attempts to prevent a détente in Europe have not ceased. All the states of this continent will still have to make serious efforts to bring about the convocation of an all-European conference.

An improvement of the situation on the continent naturally requires that the Soviet-West-German and the Polish-West-German treaties should enter into force as soon as possible.

There should also be a settlement of the problems connected with West Berlin. If the USA, France and Britain proceed, as we have done, from respect for the allied agreements which determine the special status of West Berlin, from respect for the sovereign rights of the GDR as an independent socialist state, the current negotiations could be successfully completed to the mutual advantage of all the parties concerned, including the West Berlin population itself.

Another pressing task is establishment of equitable relations between the GDR and the FRG, based on the generally accepted rules of international law, and also admission of both these states to the United Nations.

Considerable importance should also be attached to the satisfaction of the legitimate demand of the Czechoslovak Socialist Republic that the Munich Agreement should be recognised as having been invalid from the outset.

Comrades, disarmament is one of the most important international problems of our day. We seek to secure concrete results reducing the danger of war, and to prevent the peoples from accepting the arms race as an inevitable evil.

A treaty on the non-proliferation of nuclear weapons was prepared and has entered into force in the period under review. Although far from all states, including some of the nuclear powers, have yet acceded to it, it does to a certain extent narrow down the danger of an outbreak of nuclear war. The important point now is to have the FRG, Japan, Italy and other countries back up their signatures to the treaty with its ratification.

Treaties banning the stationing of nuclear weapons in outer space and on the sea- and ocean-floor have been concluded. But what has been achieved constitutes only the first few steps. It is our aim to bring about a situation in which nuclear energy shall serve peaceful purposes only.

We are engaged in negotiations with the USA on a limitation of strategic armaments. Their favourable outcome would make it possible to avoid another round in the missile arms race, and to release considerable resources for constructive purposes. We are seeking to have the negotiations produce positive results.

However, I should like to emphasize that disarmament talks in general, to say nothing of those involving discussion of highly delicate military-technical aspects, can be productive only if equal consideration is given to the security interests of the parties, and if no one seeks to obtain unilateral advantages.

The struggle for an end to the arms race, both in nuclear and conventional weapons, and for disarmament—all the way to general and complete disarmament—will continue to be one of the most important lines in the foreign-policy activity of the CPSU and the Soviet state.

In recent years, the USSR's relations with the countries of the capitalist world have been fairly active and diverse. With some of them co-operation has been extended on general foreign-policy issues, and political consultations promoting better mutual understanding have been accepted in practice. Economic, scientific and technical ties, in some instances resting on a long-term basis, have acquired considerable scale. For instance, we have been co-operating—on mutually advantageous terms, of course—with Italy in building the Volzhsky Auto Works, and with Austria and several other countries in developing the gas industry, including the laying of gas pipelines from the Soviet Union to Western Europe. Agreement was recently reached on the Soviet Union's participation in setting up an iron-and-steel complex in France. Japanese companies are to co-operate in building a new port in the Far East. Other major projects, in which our business partners have displayed a keen interest, are at the discussion stage.

As usual, we have devoted much attention to our relations with our neighbours. Good neighbourliness and co-operation with Finland have continued to grow stronger; our relations with Afghanistan and Iran have been developing successfully; we have normal relations with Pakistan and Turkey; our ties with Sweden are stable.

Our friendly relations with India have developed considerably. The Indian Government's pursuit of a peaceable, independent line in international affairs, and the traditional feelings of friendship linking the peoples of the two countries have all helped to deepen Soviet-Indian co-operation.

We believe there are considerable possibilities for further extending mutually advantageous co-operation with Japan, although the attempts by some Japanese circles to exploit the so-called territorial question have naturally done nothing to benefit Soviet-Japanese relations. Their complete normalisation on an appropriate contractual basis is also being hampered by the existence of foreign military bases in Japan. The fact is that such normalisation would be in line with the long-term interests of the peoples of the two countries, and the interests of peace in the Far East and in the Pacific area.

Now about the Soviet Union's relations with the United States of America. An improvement of Soviet-American relations would be in the interests of the Soviet and the American peoples, the interests of stronger peace. However, we cannot pass over the US aggressive actions in various parts of the world. In the recent period, the US Administration has taken a more rigid stance on a number of international issues, including some which have a bearing on the interests of the Soviet Union. The frequent zigzags in US foreign policy, which are apparently connected with some kind of domestic political moves from short-term considerations, have also made dealings with the United States much more difficult.

We proceed from the assumption that it is possible to improve relations between the USSR and the USA. Our principled line with respect to the capitalist countries, including the USA, is consistently and fully to practise the principles of peaceful coexistence, to develop mutually advantageous ties, and to co-operate, with states prepared to do so, in strengthening peace, making our relations with them as stable as possible. But we have to consider whether we are dealing with a real desire to settle outstanding issues at the negotiation table or attempts to conduct a "positions of strength" policy.

Whenever the imperialists need to cover up their aggressive schemes, they try to revive the "Soviet menace" myth. They seek to find evidence of this threat in the depths of the Indian Ocean and on the peaks of the Cordilleras. And, of course, nothing but Soviet divisions prepared for a leap against the West are to be discovered on the plains of Europe if these are viewed through NATO field-glasses.

But the peoples will not be deceived by the attempts to ascribe to the Soviet Union intentions which are alien to it. We declare with a full sense of responsibility: we have no territorial claims on anyone whatsoever, we threaten no one, and have no intention to attack anyone, we stand for the free and independent development of all nations. But let no one, for his part, try to talk to us in terms of ultimatums and strength.

We have everything necessary—a genuine peace policy, military might and the unity of Soviet people—to ensure the inviolability of our borders against any encroachments, and to defend the gains of socialism.

Comrades, the period under review marked the end of the

quarter-century since the rout of Hitler Germany and milita-rist Japan. The fruits of that great victory still live in interna-tional realities today. The Soviet people cherish everything that has been attained at such great cost.

For more than 25 years now, our people have lived in peace. We regard this as the greatest achievement of our Party's foreign policy. For a quarter-century now, mankind has been safeguarded from world war. That is another historic achieve-ment of the peoples to which the Soviet Union and its foreign policy have made a considerable contribution. However, the forces of aggression and militarism may have been pushed back, but they have not been rendered harmless. In the post-war years, they have started more than 30 wars and armed conflicts of varying scale. Nor is it possible to consider the threat of another world war as being completely eliminated. It is the vital task of all the peaceable states, of all the peoples, to prevent this threat from becoming reality.

*The Soviet Union has countered the aggressive policy of imperialism with its policy of active defence of peace and strengthening of international security.* The main lines of this policy are well known. Our Party, our Soviet state, in co-opera-tion with the fraternal socialist countries and other peace-loving states, and with the wholehearted support of many mil-lions of people throughout the world, have now for many years been waging a struggle on these lines, taking a stand for the cause of peace and friendship among nations. The CPSU re-gards the following as the *basic* concrete tasks of this struggle in the present situation.

*First.*

To eliminate the hotbeds of war in South-East Asia and in the Middle East and to promote a political settlement in these areas on the basis of respect for the legitimate rights of states and peoples subjected to aggression.

To give an immediate and firm rebuff to any acts of ag-gression and international arbitrariness. For this, full use must also be made of the possibilities of the United Nations.

Repudiation of the threat or use of force in settling outstanding issues must become a law of international life. For its part, the Soviet Union invites the countries which accept this approach to conclude appropriate bilateral or regional treaties.

*Second.*

To proceed from the final recognition of the territorial changes that took place in Europe as a result of the Second World War. To bring about a radical turn towards a détente and peace on this continent. To ensure the convocation and success of an all-European conference.

To do everything to ensure collective security in Europe. We reaffirm the readiness expressed jointly by the participants in the defensive Warsaw Treaty to have a simultaneous annulment of this treaty and of the North Atlantic alliance, or—as a first step—dismantling of their military organisations.

*Third.*

To conclude treaties putting a ban on nuclear, chemical, and bacteriological weapons.

To work for an end to the testing of nuclear weapons, including underground tests, by everyone everywhere.

To promote the establishment of nuclear-free zones in various parts of the world.

We stand for the nuclear disarmament of all states in possession of nuclear weapons, and for the convocation for these purposes of a conference of the five nuclear powers—the USSR, the USA, the PRC, France and Britain.

*Fourth.*

To invigorate the struggle to halt the race in all types of weapons. We favour the convocation of a world conference to consider disarmament questions to their full extent.

We stand for the dismantling of foreign military bases. We stand for a reduction of armed forces and armaments in areas where the military confrontation is especially dangerous, above all in Central Europe.

We consider it advisable to work out measures reducing the probability of accidental outbreak or deliberate fabrication of armed incidents and their development into international crises, into war.

The Soviet Union is prepared to negotiate agreements on reducing military expenditure, above all by the major powers.

*Fifth.*

The UN decisions on the abolition of the remaining colonial regimes must be fully carried out. Manifestations of racism and apartheid must be universally condemned and boycotted.

*Sixth.*

The Soviet Union is prepared to deepen relations of mutually advantageous co-operation in every sphere with states which for their part seek to do so. Our country is prepared to participate together with the other states concerned in settling problems like the conservation of the environment, development of power and other natural resources, development of transport and communications, prevention and eradication of the most dangerous and widespread diseases, and the exploration and development of outer space and the world ocean.

Such are the main features of the programme for the struggle for peace and international co-operation, for the freedom and independence of nations, which our Party has put forward.

And we declare that, while consistently pursuing its policy of peace and friendship among nations, the Soviet Union will continue to conduct a resolute struggle against imperialism, and firmly to rebuff the evil designs and subversions of aggressors. As in the past, we shall give undeviating support to the peoples' struggle for democracy, national liberation and socialism.

Comrades, it is clear from what has been said that the past five years have been a period of vigorous and intense activity by our Party and state in the sphere of international policy.

Of course, in international affairs not everything depends on us or our friends alone. We have not advanced in every sphere as fast as we should like towards the goals we set ourselves. A number of important acts have yet to be brought to completion, and their importance will become fully evident later. But the overall balance is obvious: great results have been achieved in these five years. Our country's international position has become even stronger, its prestige has been enhanced, and the Soviet people's peaceful endeavour has reliable protection.

# Part IV

THE INTERESTS OF THE PEOPLE,
CONCERN FOR THEIR WELL-BEING—
THE SUPREME AIM OF THE PARTY'S ACTIVITIES

Dear comrades! Dear Muscovites!

The working people of the Baumansky Constituency have conferred a great honour on me. They have again nominated me candidate to the Supreme Soviet of the Russian Federation. Permit me to thank the employees of the organizations and establishments that have nominated me, all those comrades—both Communists and non-Party people, both veterans of labour and the young people who will be performing their important civic duty for the first time this year—taking part in the elections of the bodies of Soviet power. I would like to express my sincere thanks to the persons endowed with your confidence who have spoken here at this meeting, to the canvassers and all the other comrades who have worked so hard during the election campaign.

I regard this as a sign of your confidence in the Party above all, in its efforts and struggle, its aims and purposes. These aims and plans of the Party, comrades, are the aims and plans of the whole of our people, all Soviet people.

At pre-election meetings it is usually the custom to report on the results of the work accomplished in the period following the previous elections. However, today it appears as if we are all well-informed about these results. The 24th Party Congress which closed its proceedings but two months ago, and which was held in this very hall, considered from all angles the results of the splendid labour efforts of our people in the preceding five-year period. We are rightfully proud of these results. At the same time we regard them as a point of departure for progress towards new achievements of a higher order.

Our path of advance, and the general line of our development for the next five-year period and for a longer term than that, have been determined by the decisions of the Congress. As you know, the purpose of these decisions is to ensure a considerably higher material and cultural level in the living standards of the people on the basis of a high rate of development of socialist production, higher efficiency, greater scientific and technological progress and an accelerated growth of labour productivity.

In other words, the 24th CPSU Congress has oriented the economy of the country in all its sectors, and it has instructed all the leading bodies and personnel of the Party and state to work on improving the standard of living of the people. We have never set such goals on such a broad plane before.

The interests of the people, their well-being, and their spiritual and cultural development, constitute the primary concern of the Party. The Party itself was founded to take care of these things. The Revolution was carried out for this purpose. For these ends the Soviet people courageously surmounted tremendous difficulties and made great sacrifices. Today we can say with pride that our struggle and our efforts have borne fruit. The heroic Soviet people have triumphed over all the difficulties. They have now come out onto a broad and bright road led by the Party of Lenin—the road to communism. To borrow the words of a well-known revolutionary song, they are forging the keys of happiness. And this happiness, which has been built up by the people themselves, will be the best reward to many generations of fighters for our communist cause.

The target figures of the Ninth Five-Year Plan adopted by the 24th Party Congress are indeed impressive. We shall build hundreds of new factories and plants, giant electric power stations and long transport arteries. Besides, our plans provide for the re-equipment and reconstruction of several thousand enterprises built at an earlier time, for the comprehensive introduction of new equipment and new production techniques. We shall also build many blocks of flats, schools, hospitals, stadiums and houses of culture.

There are serious problems which have to be solved in the countryside too. It is essential to ensure a sizable increase in crop yields and livestock productivity, to expand the work for improving the living conditions of the state farm workers and collective farmers. There are many tasks ahead of us. It should be pointed out that these tasks are very important and, in general, not easy. The countryside will be able to cope with these tasks only if it is assisted by the town, i.e. if the working class produces the farm machinery, fertilizers, herbicides and many other material and technical means which are needed. Boosting the output of farm products is the concern of the entire Soviet people.

In short, comrades, it is necessary for all of us to work hard to accomplish the plans we have outlined. We have jobs enough for all—for our glorious working class, for our collective farmers and for our intellectuals.

The course set by the Congress has met with the full understanding and support of the Soviet people. The working people of town and countryside have readily responded to the call of the Party to step up their activity in the upbuilding of communism. They are helping to carry out the decisions of the Congress of the Leninist Party with their conscientious labour effort.

The Soviet scientists have responded to the decisions of the Congress with outstanding achievements, particularly in the field of space research and exploration of the celestial bodies. In addition to the diligent moon-rover which is still functioning on the Moon, in addition to our two automatic stations which are proceeding to Mars, we have now launched the world's first orbital manned station—the *Salyut*. It has already received two guests: the spaceships *Soyuz-10* and *Soyuz-11*. The gallant crew of the station—the cosmonauts Georgi Dobrovolski, Vladislav Volkov and Viktor Patsayev—have been working successfully, conducting important research for the benefit of the Soviet people and the whole of mankind. Comrades, the undertaking is an impressive demonstration of our mighty industrial potential, and of the possibilities of our technology and science which will make a very big contribution to the accomplishment of the great programme of development of the USSR outlined by the Congress.

In the last few weeks pre-election meetings have been held in practically every inhabited locality of our boundless country. Tens of thousands, hundreds of thousands of people have addressed these meetings. The people have instructed their candidates to do their best to fulfil the new five-year plan, to carry out the decisions of the 24th CPSU Congress.

Here at this meeting with the voters of the Baumansky District of Moscow, I must say a few kind words about the working people of our capital. Muscovites have long been in the lead in the promotion of the All-Union competitive production effort in the socialist spirit. In the last few years they have introduced quite a few invaluable proposals which have won nation-wide recognition and support. And now, in the early months of the new five-year period, the Muscovites have proposed a drive for the accomplishment of the production plans for the current year of 1971 ahead of schedule. This initiative has been supported by thousands of collectives in our country fully in keeping with the glorious traditions of the working people of the capital.

It is pleasant to note that the workers, engineers, technicians and office employees of the Baumansky District occupy a worthy place among the advanced workers. Last year the working people of the Baumansky District fulfilled the industrial output plan by September 30. They have made a good start this year too. In the competitive production drive, the enterprises of the district have put out several million roubles' worth of products above the planned targets. Comrades, I would like to wish you all success in living up to your pledges in the first year of the five-year period. I am sure you will manage to do more than you have undertaken to do.

It is particularly important that, at the Moscow enterprises, including those of your district, there is an increasing number of first-class teams and sections. In upholding the honour of the capital, the honour of the Moscow trade mark, the workers of the city have shown that they fully understand the ideas of the 24th CPSU Congress and are doing their best to put them into practice. Conscientious efficient labour contributed by each worker, coupled with high quality of the products, is the key to the solution of the big problems confronting us in the new five-year period. This will raise the level of the national economy, and the level of our whole life. This is the only way for us to achieve a real and sizable improvement in the standard of living of the working people. And the Soviet people, headed by the Party, are confidently advancing along this way from which we shall not deviate.

Comrades, the day after tomorrow the people will elect the new deputies to the Supreme Soviets of the Union and Autonomous Republics, of the territorial, regional, area, city, district, village and settlement Soviets too. The deputies will receive a mandate for the management of society's affairs for the next few years.

It is not difficult to imagine the tremendous volume of work that will have to be shouldered by the newly elected Soviets. They will play a very big part in boosting output both in towns and countryside. The implementation of the plans for the construction of blocks of flats, schools and children's establishments, for the introduction of local amenities and improvements, and for providing the working people with the necessary commodities and services, is the direct concern of the Soviets.

Can we overlook such questions as the organization of the leisure of the working people, and the development of the network of sports, travel, cultural and other service facilities? These matters are in large measure also the concern of the Soviets.

There is no need to list here all the important problems in whose solution the Soviets will have to play a decisive part. However, it is important to point out that the local authorities will have to shoulder a considerable share of the work in implementing the decisions adopted by the 24th Congress of our Party. Today herein lies the main contribution of the Soviets to the consolidation and development of the new socialist way of life.

It is now easier for the Soviets to cope with the problems and tasks confronting them. Legislative acts passed in the recent years have extended the scope of powers enjoyed by the Soviets as the supreme bodies of state power in the localities. These legislative acts have also expanded the material and financial possibilities of the Soviets. As well, the enterprises, institutions and organizations providing services to the population have been put under the jurisdiction of the Soviets. The Soviets now have the right to co-ordinate the work of the enterprises located on their territory, in particular to organize the production of mass consumer items. The Soviets are now in a position to do a lot in stimulating the work of the local industries, organising co-operative workshops and different handicrafts.

In short, the Soviets are now in a position to do for the voters what the latter expect of them. But, of course, in doing this, the Soviets should make correct use of the means they have at their disposal and of the rights they enjoy.

Members of the public have pointed out more than once that in many cases the Soviets fail to utilise fully the material and financial resources available to them, or else that they utilise them very slowly. Quite often money is used for financing projects which cannot be regarded as projects of primary importance. The Soviets do not always take advantage of their right to pool the funds of enterprises and organizations allocated for the construction of housing, cultural and service establishments. The result is that the living conditions of the people are not improved as fast as they should be. We cannot put up with that, comrades. The newly elected Soviets should take decisive steps to overcome these shortcomings.

The Soviets can do a great deal with the funds secured in excess of their plans for budgetary income or with funds that have been saved. However, it should also be pointed out that there have been cases when funds, which by law should be spent by the Soviets, have been withdrawn by higher local government bodies. This is an infringement of the rights of the Soviets. Such action hampers the initiative of the local government workers. More than that, it leaves them with a feeling of just resentment against those who violate our laws in such a manner. Comrades, there should be no cases of this kind.

Since we are discussing the unrealised possibilities of the Soviets, I would like to recall the following case. The Central Committee Report to the 24th CPSU Congress pointed out that we have many people, such as pensioners, housewives and disabled persons who would have gladly worked to the measure of their strength in the services sphere on a co-operative basis, for instance. To enlist the services of these people in socially useful work, to mobilize their activity is one of the tasks confronting the Soviets.

It is obvious that this activity should be governed by appropriate legal regulations. If such regulations do not exist it will be necessary to elaborate them. The important thing is to render all possible support to initiative aimed at promoting the welfare of society and at improving the work in the sphere of services.

It would be a good thing if Muscovites were to display initiative in this undertaking. Perhaps it would be a good idea for each district Soviet of the capital to organize several co-operative tailor's shops, dining-rooms and other similar enterprises. This would make it possible to find out the pros and cons of such an undertaking and then to sum up the experience accumulated and to draw pertinent conclusions of a broader nature.

And now a few words about the style and methods of work of our Soviets. The Soviets, particularly the local Soviets, are precisely those authorities with which the ordinary Soviet citizen comes into contact most often. The working people go to the Soviets about matters concerning their daily needs. They go to the Soviets when they want to get an answer to some question or another, or to solve some problem.

The people who work in the Soviets—i.e. local government bodies—are good, conscientious and competent people who like their jobs. They display concern for all the aspects of life in their district or settlement. However, it is a fact that there are still unfortunate exceptions to this rule. It sometimes happens that when a citizen comes to his local Soviet he does not get the welcome that he is entitled to expect. Ill-will is shown towards him and his problem remains unsolved. And if they do solve his problem, they first make him come several times, i.e. they make him haunt their threshold.

We still have comrades who regard receiving visitors who come about their personal affairs as a thing of minor importance which does not warrant special attention. They say they have more important matters on their hands. Of course, the people who work in the Soviets have a lot on their hands. However, the attitude they display to the needs of the people, including personal needs, is not a thing of minor importance. This attitude is an important indicator of the level of the work at the given Soviet.

I would like to remind you that Lenin repeatedly drew attention to the need to conduct a persistent struggle against bureaucratic distortions in the work of the bodies of Soviet power. The Soviets, supported by the Party organizations, should persistently struggle against such distortions.

The decisions of the 24th Congress say that the work of the Soviets will be effective only if it is widely supported by the people as a whole. There are already several million voluntary activists working in the Soviets and their numbers are growing all the time. This is a good and important indication of the truly democratic character of the work in the Soviets. But enlisting large numbers of activists around the Soviets does not mean that this will solve all the problems. Far from it.

The object is to ensure constant contact between the Soviets and all the voters. The decision of the CPSU Central Committee of March 5, 1971, points out the need to ensure this. It says that the population, the voters, should be kept informed of all the practical affairs of the Soviets, and that they should take an active part in the measures taken by the Soviets. The most important matters bearing on the life of the districts and towns should be submitted for discussion by the working people at the enterprises and at their places of residence. It is the direct duty of the deputies now being elected to make this a rule in the work of the Soviets.

The essence of socialist democracy consists in drawing the broadest possible masses of working people into active participation in social affairs. And who, if not the Soviets in the first place, should implement this principle of people's power under socialism?

It is important to stress at this point what we have repeatedly said before: in their big and important job, our Soviets and their staffs should receive the constant assistance and support of all Party organizations. It is the duty of the Communists to do everything necessary to improve the work of the Soviets and to infuse it with life.

The Soviets are our own people's power. This power was born in the flames of revolution. The Great October Revolution triumphed under the slogan: "All power to the Soviets!" Soviet power secured the victory of socialism in our country. And the whole activity of the Soviets today is subordinated to the achievement of the greatest historical task—the task of building communism.

Vladimir Ilyich Lenin, by his own example, showed us the concern that Communists should show for the Soviets, and for constantly increasing the part they play in the life of the people. So let us, comrades, in this matter, too, worthily carry on the work of Lenin!

Comrades, since all of us on Sunday will take part in electing the highest body of authority of the Russian Federation—the Supreme Soviet of the RSFSR—it is appropriate at this point to touch upon certain issues connected with the further development of the Russian Soviet Federative Socialist Republic.

I have chanced to be in many Union Republics these last few years, and everywhere—in the Ukraine and in Georgia, in Kazakhstan and Armenia, in Byelorussia and Azerbaijan—everywhere the people spoke with great warmth, with respect and affection about the Russian people, and about the contribution of the Russian Federation to the development of all the republics of our country. These sincere words of gratitude have been merited by the working class, the farm workers and the intelligentsia of Soviet Russia. Their labour, their determination and knowledge, their self-sacrifice and heartfelt generosity have played a vital part in the practical implementation of the Party's national policy, in the transformation of former backward outlying territories of tsarist Russia into flourishing socialist republics.

In the constellation of the republics, equal in rights, the RSFSR holds a leading place—by the size of its population and of its territory, by its natural wealth, and by its economic and scientific-technological potential.

The working people of the Russian Federation successfully fulfilled the tasks of the Eighth Five-Year Plan. In the course of five years, production assets and the output of industrial goods increased by 50 per cent. There was also a rise in the growth rate of agricultural production. The gross annual output of agriculture in the 1966–1970 period was 20 per cent higher than in the previous five-year period.

All this is very good, comrades, but the assignments of the Ninth Five-Year Plan, the targets for a more distant future demand a further and faster advance on a broader front than before. Experience teaches us that the broader this front and the greater the number of tasks which have to be tackled simultaneously, the more imperative the need to solve them co-operatively, systematically and purposefully, taking into account the complex and varied relationships between different areas of the country, between different sectors of the national economy, and between all spheres of social life. In other words, what is necessary is a many-sided, systematic approach towards the elaboration of major decisions. We have adopted such an attitude and shall consistently translate it into life.

Not so long ago, for instance, the Politbureau of the Central Committee examined the question of measures for the development of agriculture in the Smolensk Region. We tried to approach the problem on a wide scale and to solve it, taking into consideration the requirements of all sectors of agriculture, and their ties with industry, transport, trade, etc. The Central Committee's decision, therefore, embraces such matters as the improvement of elevator, refrigerator and storage facilities, the erection of power transmission lines and sub-stations, the construction of a casting-yard for reinforced-concrete parts and a plant manufacturing large panels for housing construction, the training of skilled personnel, and many other things.

It is important to continue to expand the practice of a comprehensive examination of the state of affairs in groups of regions of the Russian Federation, for instance, the Central-Black Earth zone, the North-West area, the European North, the Volga area, the Urals, and others. Special attention ought to be given to such problems as land improvement, a further rise in agricultural crop yields, the development of livestock farming, road construction, amenities in the countryside, and the future of small towns.

I would like to dwell particularly on the questions of a more intensive development of natural resources and of the economic potential of Siberia and the Far East. Speaking about plan assignments, in the period of the new five-year plan the share of the eastern areas in the Russian Federation's production should rise from 11.8 to 31.5 per cent in oil extraction, from 13.4 to 45.4 per cent in gas extraction, from 58.2 to 64.5 per cent in coal extraction, and from 22.4 to 31.3 per cent in pulp production.

But this is only the quantitative side of the matter. No matter how important the quoted indicators may be in themselves, it is no less important how, in what way, and by what methods it is planned to solve such a big and important task as the further development of the eastern areas of the RSFSR. As an example I can refer to the recently-adopted decision on measures for the all-round development, between 1971 and 1980, of the productive forces of Krasnoyarsk Territory.

These measures envisage the construction of large-capacity power stations and the setting up, on this foundation, of a new base of the power industry and power-consuming enterprises, including the East Siberian electro-metallurgical works; the launching of a large-scale petrochemical complex; the better use of timber resources; a noticeable growth of agricultural production and development of enterprises of light industry and the food industry; the establishment of scientific institutions. Naturally, along with this, it is planned to build houses and schools, cultural centres and municipal and public services.

Decisions of this nature and scale, binding together factors of a most diverse character—economic, socio-political, demographic, geographic, and many others—should be drawn up. This should be done in particular on the Bratsk economic complex, the Sayany territorial-production complex, and the West Siberian oil base. It is necessary later to start to elaborate similar comprehensive programmes of development for Yakutia, the Chukchi Peninsula and all the other areas of the Far East and Siberia.

In posing such a task, the Party is relying on the Siberian division and Far Eastern branch of the USSR Academy of Sciences. The matter, after all, concerns a truly scientific approach to the development of immense territories of the Russian Federation, an approach that would combine the carrying out of urgent tasks of the present time with consideration for the long-range prospects of development of the country. We must work today in such a way that our children and grandchildren will be able to add more and more new storeys to the edifice which we are building, and not have to re-do what has already been done.

Let us be frank, comrades, these immense projects cannot be completely carried out in one five-year period or even two. But by mobilising existing resources and leaning on local initiative, we can accomplish a great deal straight away.

Permit me to express confidence that the Communists and the working people of the multinational Russian Federation will successfully carry out the historic decisions of the 24th Congress of the Party and make a worthy contribution to the further progress of our great socialist country.

Comrades, all of us, Muscovites, are proud of living and working in our wonderful city. The aim that the capital of the Union of Soviet Socialist Republics should become still more beautiful and well-appointed is one of the objectives constantly before the Party.

Back in 1935 the Central Committee of the All-Union Communist Party (Bolsheviks) and the Council of People's Commissars of the USSR endorsed a master-plan for the reconstruction of Moscow. This was the first social and town-planning document of such a scale in world history. Under this plan, which was clarified and supplemented in subsequent years, the appearance of the ancient Russian capital changed considerably. In the years of Soviet power the population of Moscow has almost quadrupled and now totals more than 7 million. In the same period, city housing has increased nearly six times. Industrial output has gone up more than 100 times. Beautiful avenues and thoroughfares have been made, and splendid buildings erected. Eighty-nine Metro stations have been built. Today Moscow is actually one of the best-appointed capitals of the world.

However, the complicated and quickened rhythm of urban life and the rapid growth of the requirements of the population are making further demands. Our aim is to transform Moscow into a model communist city, well laid out, with modern architecture, and having public amenities and sanitary and hygienic facilities of a high standard. The other day, as you know, the Central Committee of the Party and the Council of Ministers of the USSR approved the main proposals of a new master-plan for the development of Moscow and a forest-park protection belt. This plan, which was published in the papers yesterday, covers a period up to 1985–1990 with longer-range prospects taken into account.

At one time, in the early years of Soviet power, Lenin, in a conversation with architects, said that Moscow should be re-built in such a way that it would be artistic and, at the same time, a comfortable place to live in. The new master-plan is aimed at carrying out this instruction of Lenin's. It is based on the use of the latest achievements in city-building, and, at the same time, on preserving the distinctive, historically-evolved appearance of Moscow. It is a blend of doubled pro-duction of the capital's industrial enterprises with considerable improvement of the working and living conditions, and rec-reational facilities of the working people.

The task in hand now is to translate this plan into life. Nat-urally, the whole country will take part in the development of the capital, but the main tasks are to be carried out by the Muscovites, by the Party and YCL organizations of the city, by the trade unions, the Moscow Soviet, and district Soviets of the capital. It goes without saying that considerable work also lies ahead of all Communists and of all the residents of the Baumansky District.

I hope that the Muscovites will cope with these tasks with honour. I would advise you, comrades, to demand more from your Deputies—those in the districts, in the Moscow Soviet, and in the Supreme Soviet of the Republic. Let our Soviets, our Deputies constantly feel that their work in carrying out the Congress decisions and the assignments of the five-year plan is always under the control of the electorate. Nothing but good will come from this, I am sure.

Comrades, practical work in promoting the political line of the 24th CPSU Congress embraces not only internal problems of development of the country, but also our foreign policy.

The 24th Congress reaffirmed that the outstanding features of the Soviet Union's foreign policy are purposefulness and consistency, and an approach to the solution of current prob-lems keeping the long-range targets and tasks in view. As be-fore, we shall do everything possible to promote co-operation among the socialist countries, and the consolidation of the world socialist system. As before, we shall strengthen our militant alliance and friendship with the young national democratic states, and with all forces of the anti-imperialist movement. As before, we shall oppose aggression, and work for universal peace, and for the replacement of military blocs and groupings by systems of collective security.

Only two months have passed since the Congress, but we have made definite steps forward in all the main directions of foreign policy activity. Speaking of most recent events, the conclusion of the Treaty of Friendship and Co-operation with the United Arab Republic should be mentioned first of all. The contents of this Treaty vividly reflect the close friendship, mutual support and understanding which distinguish the relations of the Soviet Union with progressive Arab states. We regard this document as one more proof of the growing unity of the anti-imperialist front of the peoples of the world.

The outcome of the visit to the Soviet Union of Canadian Prime Minister Trudeau also deserves mention. The Soviet-Canadian protocol on consultations, like the Soviet-French protocol, signed earlier, at the time of the visit to the USSR of President Pompidou of France, convincingly shows the great possibilities of active political co-operation among states with differing social systems. The greater the interest manifested by our partners in maintaining peace, in developing economic, scientific-technological and other ties, the greater will be the possibility of achieving these goals.

This also applies in full measure to such a major issue of the times as stopping the arms race. In view of its tremendous importance, permit me to dwell in detail on certain questions concerning this matter.

The struggle against militarism and for disarmament has always, since Lenin's time, been an inalienable component of the foreign policy activities of the Soviet state. Our country and our Party adhere to this course today, too. One more proof of this are the documents of the 24th Congress, which formulate a whole set of concrete proposals aimed both at the adoption of partial measures and at the creation of foundations for general and complete disarmament.

They may say that the Soviet state advanced proposals of this kind in the past and that they were not accepted by the other side. Does this not mean that disarmament plans, and plans to limit the arms drive are unfeasible in a world where capitalism still exists, and where the imperialist powers continue to exert considerable influence on the international situation?

It stands to reason that the fight for disarmament is a complicated matter. In this, as in many other foreign policy issues, we come up against the stubborn resistance of the imperialist forces. Nevertheless, we regard the proposals set forth by the 24th CPSU Congress, not as slogans of propaganda, but as slogans of action, mirroring political aims which are becoming increasingly attainable in our epoch.

What is it that permits us to raise the question in such a manner? First and foremost, the changed correlation of forces in the world—both socio-political and military forces.

Only a few years ago, the imperialists, and primarily, the US imperialists, seriously hoped, with the help of an arms race, to strengthen their position on the world scene, and, at the same time, to weaken the economy of the USSR and other socialist countries, and frustrate our plans of peaceful construction. The failure of these calculations of our enemies has now become most obvious. Everybody now sees that socialism is powerful enough to secure both reliable defences and economic development, though, of course, without large expenditures on defence, we would have been able to push our economy ahead much faster.

On the other hand, the imperialists, including those in the United States, the richest capitalist country, are themselves increasingly feeling the negative economic and political consequences of an all-out arms drive. Enormous military spending engenders in the capitalist countries chronic inflation, causes systematic currency and financial crises, and hampers the solution of the worsening internal problems.

Simultaneously, indignation is mounting among the working people over the policy of militarism and aggression. The anti-war movement in the United States is assuming an increasingly mass character and is bringing serious pressure to bear on the government. Resistance to the growth of military expenditure is also increasing in other NATO countries. As a result, even among some of the ruling circles of Western states, the arms race is no longer being regarded as an undiluted blessing. All this, of course, to a certain degree helps the socialist and other peace-loving countries in their efforts to combat the arms race. This fight against the arms race is becoming a more realistic proposition.

This atmosphere undoubtedly adds significance to the Soviet-American talks on the limitation of strategic arms, a positive outcome of which would, in our opinion, be in the interests of the people of both countries, and would help to consolidate universal peace.

I have mentioned before that the determining factor for the success of these negotiations is strict observance of the principle of equal security for both sides, and rejection of any attempts to gain unilateral advantages at the expense of the other side. I would therefore like to hope that the government of the United States, too, will adopt a constructive attitude.

Washington pays lip service to the principle of equal security, but the American side cannot bring itself to consistently promote this in practice. For instance, an uproar is systematically raised in the United States—especially on the eve of the adoption in Washington of a new military budget—over Soviet defence programmes. The measures which we take to strengthen our defences are pictured in this campaign almost as some kind of "perfidy," as a direct threat to the success of the talks. But, we ask, on what grounds does Washington expect us to reject already-adopted programmes, when the US Government itself, throughout the period of negotiations has adopted several major decisions on the build-up of its strategic forces? It is high time to reject such double standards when assessing one's own moves and the moves of the other side.

And this refers not only to missiles. The US propaganda machine has made much fuss about the Soviet Navy. Washington regards it as a threat that our naval vessels should appear in the Mediterranean, in the Indian Ocean, and in other seas, whereas American politicians regard it as normal and natural that their Sixth Fleet should be constantly stationed in the Mediterranean, nextdoor to the Soviet Union, you might say, and the Seventh Fleet—off the coasts of China and Indo-China.

We have never regarded it as an ideal situation for navies of great powers to remain for long periods far from home waters. We are ready to settle this problem, too, but to settle it on an equal footing.

The Soviet Union is ready, on the basis of such principles, to discuss any proposals. We, on our part, came forward at the Congress with a number of initiatives such as the banning of all types of mass-destruction weapons, the curtailment of the military budgets of states, and the total discontinuation of nuclear weapons tests. We also proposed the convocation of a conference of the five nuclear powers—the Soviet Union, the People's Republic of China, the United States, Britain and France. We are waiting for an answer to these proposals. The world public is also waiting for it.

You know that among our proposals there is one on reducing armed forces and armaments in Europe. This is a major and independent question, and one on which we and our allies have repeatedly made appropriate suggestions. Practical steps in working for its settlement would be of great importance for a detente and a lasting peace in Europe. It can be noted with satisfaction that the Soviet Union's point of view on this question has been met with definite interest in most countries of the West. The recent NATO session in Lisbon also had to take up this matter, but we still have no clear answer. We continue to be asked: does our proposal concern only foreign armed forces or does it also involve national armed forces? We could answer that as follows: We are ready to discuss both aspects. We, on our part, reaffirm our readiness to give due attention to all these important questions. Naturally, we shall act in close contact with our allies.

Permit me, comrades, to assure you that the Central Committee of the CPSU and the Soviet Government, loyal to the 24th Party Congress decisions, will continue perseveringly and actively to conduct a foreign policy aimed at securing all the necessary conditions for the quiet, peaceful endeavour of the Soviet people, and at strengthening the foundations of peace throughout the world. This is a Leninist foreign policy line, and we shall consistently translate it into life.

Comrades, in the approaching elections, you, the electorate of the Baumansky District of Moscow, like all Soviet electors, will be voting not only for individual people nominated as candidates for Deputy by the bloc of Communists and non-Party people. What is actually also being put to a vote is the political platform of this bloc. It is based on the decisions of the 24th Congress of the Party, a congress which has charted a clear course for the further strengthening of the might of our country, for a further rise in the living and cultural standards of the Soviet people, for the further cohesion of Soviet society and development of socialist democracy, for the fight for peace and international security. Permit me to express confidence that the elections will fully confirm the approval by the entire people of the line of our Party.

In conclusion, I wish once again to thank you for the trust you have shown me. Permit me to assure you that, as in all of my working life, I shall continue to give all my energies and strength to the cause of communism, to the people's cause. For me, as a Communist, there can be no other interests, no other aims.

Long live the indestructible unity of the Party and the people!

# Part V

SPEECH AT THE USSR RALLY OF STUDENTS
IN THE KREMLIN ON OCTOBER 20, 1971

*Wednesday, October 20, 1971*

## NATION-WIDE RALLY OF STUDENTS

Dear comrades!

Our young friends!

Allow me to congratulate you on behalf of the Central Committee of the Communist Party on the inauguration of the All-Union Rally of Students and to convey ardent greetings and the best wishes to you and to the whole many-million strong army of Soviet students.

I admit that I was happy to accept the invitation to speak at your rally. Meeting the younger generation who embodies the future of our country is always a pleasant function. This especially applies to you, the militant vanguard of the glorious Soviet students.

Your rally is taking place soon after the 24th Congress of our Party. This is not accidental.

The fulfilment of the grandiose plans mapped out by the Congress will require strenuous effort of the Party and the whole people. And here we must bear in mind that the very nature of Soviet people's labour is changing before our very eyes. The job done today by a rank-and-file worker at a plant or by a collective-farm machine operator was considered not so long ago the competence of a technician or engineer only. This is how our science and technology have advanced and how the vocational skill of the people have risen. But life is going on at a fast pace. And it makes ever higher demands of us, of every Soviet man and woman.

Our Party is well aware of all these processes.

The resolutions of the 24th Congress have put forward the paramount task of combining in the fullest and organic way the advantages of our socialist system with the achievements of the scientific and technological revolution. And this calls for the training and education of competent personnel, creating large detachments of new specialists capable of solving the ever greater and more complex problems of communist construction.

The resolutions of the 24th Congress have handed to young Soviet people the baton, as it were, of scientific, technological and social progress. The Congress urged the young people of the Soviet land to march in the front ranks of those who champion the high efficiency of production and culture of life, the fostering of communist norms in our reality.

And, of course, comrades, this appeal applies entirely to you Soviet students too. The point is that those who study at universities, institutes and secondary technical schools today are the ones who in the nearest future will be taking an active, creative part in carrying out our plans. The fulfilment of the 9th five-year plan is the common cause of the Party and of the people. And Soviet students are to make their contribution to this great cause.

The future managers of production and of extremely important research institutions and offices are sitting here, in this hall today. Present here are the future educators of new generations, the creators of new cultural values. You are the ones who will carry on the work that had been started by the generation of the October Revolution, the work that had been continued by the generation of the first Five-Year Plans, the fruits of which were heroically defended against the enemy by the soldiers of the Great Patriotic War.

In olden days, dear friends, only very few people could afford to get a higher education. You are well informed about that. It was only our socialist system that had flung the doors

1. On March 1, 1973, General Secretary of the Central Committee of the Communist Party of the Soviet Union Leonid I. Brezhnev signed Communist Party Membership Card No. 1, which was filled in the name of Vladimir I. Lenin, the founder of the party.

2. Moscow. March 30, 1971. The 24th Congress of the Communist Party of the Soviet Union. On the rostrum is General Secretary of the CPSU Central Committee Leonid I. Brezhnev.

The report he made at the Congress reflected the major points of Soviet domestic and foreign policy, defined and formulated the Soviet peace program.

3. Leonid I. Brezhnev in a shop of the Frunze engineering plant in Kirghizia. This republic, relying on the assistance of the other republics of the Soviet Union, has increased its industrial output more than 400 times over the past 50 years.

4. Leonid I. Brezhnev spent all the years of World War II in the Army in the field and he took part in many military operations, including a landing in the area of Novorossiisk.

Colonel Leonid I. Brezhnev and his frontline comrade Lieutenant Colonel Avksenty Tikhostup on the eve of the storming of Novorossiisk in 1943.

5. 1945. A parade in Moscow to mark the victory over fascism.

Leonid I. Brezhnev (second from right) is at the head of a combined regiment of the 4th Ukrainian Front.

6. Major-General Leonid I. Brezhnev, head of the political department of the 18th army. 1945.

7. 1961 opened up a new era in mankind's history—the space era. The man who made the first orbital flight around the earth—Yuri Gagarin—is presented with the badge of pilot-cosmonaut by Leonid I. Brezhnev, President of the Presidium of the USSR Supreme Soviet.

8. Moscow. January 22, 1969. A reception in the Kremlin in honor of the new space pioneers. General Secretary of the Central Committee of the Communist Party of the Soviet Union Leonid I. Brezhnev and President of the Presidium of the USSR Supreme Soviet Nikolai V. Podgorny among the cosmonauts.

9. The activities of Leonid I. Brezhnev in leading party and government posts cover a wide range of problems and duties.

10. The opening of the Lenin Memorial in Ulyanovsk on April 16, 1970. Leonid I. Brezhnev is planting a birch tree at the building where the founder of the Communist Party of the Soviet Union and the Soviet state, Vladimir I. Lenin, was born on April 22, 1870.

11. In September 1970 Leonid I. Brezhnev visited Tajikistan. He stopped at the construction site of the Nurek hydroelectric power station dam and the young town of builders, where he talked with the people.

12. General Secretary of the Central Committee of the Communist Party of the Soviet Union Leonid I. Brezhnev conversing with workers from the Frunze plant in Kirghizia. September 1970.

13. Leaders of the Communist Party of the Soviet Union and the Soviet Government at the Selkhoztekhnika '72 exhibition.

14. Visiting Bulgarian peasants.

15. The meeting in the Kremlin with Federal Republic of Germany Chancellor Willy Brandt (1970). The Soviet Union's efforts to improve the international situation in Europe resulted in the treaty between the USSR and the FRG which formalized the principle of inviolability of existing European frontiers.

16. Moscow. May 26, 1972. General Secretary of the Central Committee of the Communist Party of the Soviet Union Leonid I. Brezhnev and American President Richard Nixon after the signing of the historic Soviet-American agreements that adopted the principle of peaceful coexistence as the cornerstone of Soviet-American relations.

17. Leonid I. Brezhnev. 1973.

of educational institutions wide open to the children of workers and peasants. They, the first Soviet students, had a hard time. Many had come to colleges and universities via workers' faculties, having learned to read and write not long before, having read but their first books, and having made their first contacts with the foundations of culture. But their passionate desire to study and to become active builders of a new world made them real specialists.

They were the first generation of the Soviet intelligentsia. Former students of workers' faculties became engineers and agronomists, teachers and doctors, Party and social workers, trade-union functionaries and diplomats. Their knowledge and efforts played an immense role in turning our country into a mighty highly-developed socialist industrial power.

In the days of the Great Patriotic War, many thousand students, putting aside their books and manuals, took up arms and joined the whole people to defend their Homeland. They had not had the time to get institute diplomas, but they won deserving diplomas of courage and heroism in the battlefields. The war prevented them from getting university graduation badges, but combat orders and medals adorned their chests.

The war was barely over when they, still wearing their tunics and greatcoats, returned to the lecture halls to finish their education. The higher schools will long remember the image of the student from the warfront. His keen sense of responsibility and industriousness, his civic passion and adherence to Party principle served as a splendid example for many subsequent generations of students.

Today the student body of our country adds up to nearly 5,000,000 students of higher educational establishments and nearly 4,500,000 students of specialised secondary and technical schools. Our Soviet student body is one flesh and blood of workers, peasants, and working intelligentsia, in other words, of those who with their labour make it possible for the youth to attain the heights of knowledge.

We can now say with a feeling of legitimate satisfaction that the system of training of cadres, set up in the years of

Soviet power, in the main meets the country's requirements, and makes it possible to provide all sectors of material production and cultural life with qualified experts.

At the dawn of socialism, Vladimir Ilyich Lenin dreamed of our country becoming one of complete literacy. This task has long been solved. We are now tackling new targets: we are completing the transition to universal secondary education. Our higher schools are also moving ahead in big strides. Just think over this one figure: by the end of the current five-year plan period, practically every tenth citizen of the USSR will have a higher school or specialised secondary school diploma. And to think that only three or four decades ago we did not even dare predict when such a time would come!

But, of course, comrades, much still has to be improved in higher education in our country. We spoke of this at the 24th Congress of our Party.

Science and its practical application in life are presently developing at such a pace that a good deal of what was even recently discovered often becomes obsolete before it finds its way to text-books and lecture courses. It is justly said that if a person, who finished higher school 15–20 years ago, did not carry on with his self-education, he would in our days find himself a worker hopelessly lagging behind everything. But this also means that work must go on efficiently and continuously as well in further improving the content and methods of teaching in the higher schools, and in strengthening the material and technical basis of higher and technical schools.

Evidently, we should likewise think of how to ensure more even staffing of higher schools with qualified scientific-pedagogic cadres, to approach more carefully the training of corresponding specialists. Optimal siting of educational institutions that would take into account the prospects of development of productive forces in different economic areas of the country and demographic factors is also of no small significance.

A good deal has been done in recent years in ensuring a greater influx of worker and peasant youth into the higher educational establishments. This approach fully stems from the

Party's policy which aims at bringing the working class, collective farm peasantry and intelligentsia closer together and strengthening the social unity of our society. Our people hailed such a major undertaking as the setting of preparatory departments at higher schools, the first graduates of which have already joined the ranks of our students.

It gives me great pleasure to tell you that the Central Committee of the Party and the Government, in conformity with the Directives of the 24th CPSU Congress, adopted an important decision the other day which provides for a sizable improvement of the material and housing conditions and amenities for students of higher and specialised secondary schools. What is meant here, specifically, is raising the size of stipends for students of higher and specialised secondary schools. The construction of a large number of new student dormitories, and substantial improvement of medical, sanatorium and spa services, in the organisation of public catering, and the development of sport centres are also envisaged. The state will allocate in the current five-year plan period an additional 1,500 million roubles alone for higher stipends and a larger number of students receiving a scholarship.

We are sure that this will further improve the training of specialists and serve as a fresh stimulus in invigorating the activity of our students, activity in carrying out the decisions of the 24th Congress of the Party, in studies and science, in work and in sports. In a word, we hold this is a justified, and "paying" investment! The important thing is that the allocated sums be used most effectively and rationally. This should be taken care of by the heads of educational establishments, corresponding ministries and departments, Party, trade union and YCL organisations.

But comrades, whichever bodies or institutions concern themselves with the successes of the higher school these successes will not come of themselves if you students yourselves do not decisively contribute towards this.

Actually speaking, your social responsibility as grown-up people begins at the moment when you step across the threshold of the higher school. For the student days mean not only preparing for the morrow, not simply awaiting it. This already means today's bright and interesting life. This means tense, creative work, and active social work.

According to the dictionary the Latin word "student" means "one devoted to learning." Indeed, the chief task of the student is to learn. This is clear to all. However, the concrete content of this concept has not remained immutable, and in our days it rapidly changes as never before. How to learn, what to learn, how to select and master the chief thing in the ocean of information relative to your profession? All these are by no means rhetorical questions.

You are preparing to become specialists at one or another section of the labour front. And your compass in studies should be the demands life makes today upon the Soviet specialist, upon the active participant in building communism.

The Soviet specialist today is a man who has well mastered the fundamentals of Marxist-Leninist teaching, who clearly sees the political aims of the Party and the country, who possesses extensive scientific and practical training and who has mastered his profession to perfection.

The Soviet specialist today is an able organiser capable of applying in practice the principles of scientific organisation of work. He is able to work with people, values the experience of the collective, listens to the opinions of comrades, and critically appraises what has been achieved.

And of course, a specialist today is a very highly cultured person, an erudite person, in general, he is a real intellectual of the new socialist society.

What is needed to attain this truly high level?

It is important, absolutely essential, to master to the full the programme material of the higher educational establishment. But this alone is not enough. It is necessary to learn to constantly perfect your knowledge, cultivate habits of a researcher and possess extensive theoretical knowledge. Without this it is hard to orientate oneself in all the increasing volume of knowledge and flood of scientific information.

The process of learning at the higher educational establishment today relies more and more upon the student's independent activities, close to research. It has become a mass phenomenon for students to take part in scientific groups and seminars; competitions and exhibitions of scientific works have become more popular than ever before. And this is very good!

I want to particularly stress, dear friends, that only by mastering Marxist-Leninist theory can one creatively acquire a profession, become an active participant in building communism, and a champion of the Party's policy among the masses. The teaching of Marxism-Leninism is the foundation, the integral part of the knowledge of a specialist in any field.

Fidelity to Marxism-Leninism and proletarian internationalism is a lofty tradition of our Party and our Komsomol, which the institutions of higher learning must strengthen and enrich in every way possible. The Soviet students are a vanguard detachment of the youth of the world. Jointly with their coevals from other countries, they actively struggle against imperialism, for social justice, for a better future for all peoples. This is a big and important asset of our students!

Comrades, your teachers help you to receive the knowledge and develop the features necessary for a Soviet specialist. We have thousands of remarkable workers: teachers, assistant professors and professors. Wherever they work, be it a famous university with a glorious history or a new institute the biography of which only begins, their efforts, experience and knowledge are a priceless capital for our society. Big scientific schools have formed in many institutions of higher learning. They are headed by the country's outstanding scholars whose names are a pride of our national and world science.

A prominent scholar, a teacher worthy of the name repeats himself in his pupils. The pupil takes over the ideological beliefs of his teacher, his attitude to work, scientific erudition and methods of work. Be worthy of your teachers, friends. Give them the highest joy which the teacher may experience: realisation of the fact that the pupil has exceeded him!

Briefly speaking, friends, Lenin's slogan: "First to learn,

secondly, to learn, and, thirdly to learn!" remains for you to-day the most important and the topical slogan of life!

However, we cannot, nor have we the right to forget about Lenin's other appeal: the appeal to ensure that the process of studies develops side by side with the process of communist education. Of course, in practice these two processes should merge into one. However, this does not come of itself. This should be taken care of and this should be done constantly both in the course of science teaching and during the organisation of social activities at the institutions of higher learning. The Party and Komsomol organisations of the institutions of higher learning must play a role of tremendous importance in this respect.

The Party organisation of the university or an institute is the political vanguard of the collective, while the Party committee of an institution of higher learning is its combat staff. In connection with granting the Party organisations of the institutions of higher learning the right to control the activities of the administration, their role in all fields of life of higher school is growing. Not a single major question pertaining to the work of an institution of higher learning should be left unnoticed by Party organisations. The contents of studies, the leisure of students, the organisation of scientific research, public activities and sport—the Communists of the institutions of higher learning should devote attention to everything.

There are not and cannot be any minor things as far as education work is concerned. This concerns one of the most complex and responsible matters—the moulding of the souls and characters, the steeling of the hearts and minds of the builders of the future!

The closer their ties with Komsomol organisations, the better they know their life and help them in their activities, the more successful the Party organisations of the institutions of higher learning will work. And this is indeed so as the Komsomol members constitute the overwhelming proportion of the Soviet students.

The work of the Komsomol organisations of the institutions

of higher learning is an important and very responsible matter. Indeed, studies at an institute or a university require of a young man a systematic approach to out-of-the-classroom studies, and what is necessary for this is a strong will and purposefulness. Comradely exactingness in respect to oneself and one's associates, strict self-discipline and a steady compliance with the main requirements of the educational procedure are the indispensable conditions for the maturing of a would-be specialist as a professional and a citizen. It is the Komsomol that must instil these features in a student. For this it is necessary to work for creating in every educational establishment of an atmosphere of creativity, enthusiasm and mutual assistance which would promote the fullest possible revelation and development of a student's abilities and would prompt him to searches, to constant advancement.

The trade union branches of the colleges have to play an increasing part in the life of the students. Concern for a proper organisation of the teaching process, for production practice, the recreation of the students, the promotion of amateur art activities, physical training and sports, for decent conditions of life in the hostels, for rendering pecuniary aid to students, and the creation of a good atmosphere of work—all this is not a trifle, comrades, but a major condition for the successful moulding and education of highly skilled specialists.

We are vitally interested in that every student grows up as a man with a clearly expressed social feeling, a man who would not imagine himself outside the collective. This, as is known, is achieved by a good and business-like organisation of volunteer work. In recent years the level of public activity in higher school has risen markedly. The Party and Young Communist League branches see to it that this activity be purposeful, diverse and interesting. Such forms of volunteer work have been found and are successfully developing which enable the youths and girls to test their abilities in the different spheres of labour and socio-political activity, while studying in colleges.

I would like to say in this connection a few kind words

about students active in public life. Enthusiastic, passionate and selfless—they are always ahead in the studies, scientific work and public affairs. The Party committees and Young Communist League branches should recommend the best of these activists for admission to the Party. We do not doubt that they will justify this high trust with honour.

I should also mention here such a comparatively new form of Young Communist League independent action as the building teams of students. In my opinion, this form of disclosing and mobilising the energies of the students and their activity fully meets the requirements of our times and the young people themselves. Over a million youths and girls have gone through the school of the "third (labour) semester." The participation in the students' building teams has sown good seeds in the souls of young people and these seeds are now yielding good sprouts.

The work of these teams proves once more that the participation of students in public life is not a game of independent action but sound and practically useful activity which gives a lot to the young people, cultivates in them the feeling of responsibility, and brings to them the recognition of society. Proof of this is that 500 students have been decorated this year alone with orders and medals for their shock work, the successes in studies and in the field of science.

It gives me particular pleasure to tell you that all the participants in the rally have been decorated with the Lenin jubilee medals for excellent study, shock work and active volunteer work.

The Central Committee of the Party heartily congratulates you on this high and deserved award.

The Central Committee of the Party is sure that all your life you will be studying, working and fighting in a Leninist manner.

Dear friends, the student period is a short one—only five to six years. Yet, it leaves a trace for the whole life. What you acquire during these years is a burden which does not lie heavy upon you. On the contrary, the greater the amount of knowledge, culture and social habits, the more confidently man feels in life.

The years of study will go by, you will pass the state examinations and defend your diploma projects, and the credit tests and projects will be left behind. But the completion of studies is only the beginning of your working career. Wherever you come to work, you will bring with you what the student years generously gave you, namely, ideological conviction, profound knowledge, love for your profession and devotion to your great homeland.

May the spirit of your student youth always live in your endeavours, affairs and dreams; may the flame of your hearts never cool down, and may your thoughts be pure and noble.

May I wish you, dear friends, excellent progress in your studies, good health, happiness and big successes in the noble work of serving the people, the lofty ideals of communism.

# Part VI

DECISIONS OF THE 24TH CPSU CONGRESS,
A PROGRAM OF ACTION FOR THE
SOVIET TRADE UNIONS

Dear comrade delegates and esteemed foreign friends,

Allow me, on behalf of the Central Committee of the Communist Party of the Soviet Union, to extend the warmest greetings to the 15th Congress of the Soviet Trade Unions. This Congress is a major event in the life of our country. It owes its significance to the important role which the trade unions, uniting in their ranks 98 million Soviet working people, play in the building of communism. It is natural, therefore, that your attention will be focused on the questions connected with the trade unions' part in carrying out the key tasks posed by the 24th Congress of the Party.

The 24th Congress of the CPSU, as we know, laid down the general lines of the home and foreign policy of the Party and Soviet state at the current stage, outlining an extensive programme for the further development of industry and agriculture, for improving living standards, and for the communist education of the working people. The resolutions of the Congress have been unanimously supported by the working class, farmers and intellectuals of the Soviet Union, and welcomed as a militant programme of action by such mass organisations as the trade unions and the Young Communist League. This nation-wide support invests the Congress resolutions with tremendous force; it inspires confidence and firm conviction that the programme mapped out by the Party Congress will be accomplished.

And this means that our Motherland will make yet another big stride forward in laying the material and technical foundations of communism, in improving social relationships, and in building up the country's economic potential and strengthening its international position. This also means that we shall accomplish the programme charted by the Congress for achieving a substantial improvement in living standards. The allocations apportioned for these purposes amount to 22,000 million roubles—more than twice the funds allocated under the past, 8th Five Year Plan.

The accomplishment of these mammoth tasks rests upon a solid material foundation. Every branch of the national economy will receive considerably more funds for development purposes than it did during the previous Five-Year Plan. The total amount of capital investments under the 9th Five-Year Plan will exceed 500,000 million roubles.

The Party pays particular attention to the development of industries immediately related to the achievement of the principal target of the Five-Year Plan—the raising of the people's living standards. Investments in agriculture will amount to 128,600 million roubles, which is 46,400 million roubles more than in the previous five-year period, and the investments in light industry and in the food, meat and dairy industries will increase by 74 per cent.

The very fact that we can afford to plan and accomplish tasks of such dimensions attests to the might and strength of the Soviet state. We have every means at our disposal—material, scientific and technological—needed for putting the allocations to good use.

Our Motherland, our Party have raised a strong army of specialists—highly skilled industrial workers, expert agricultural workers, builders, engineers and technicians, scientists and organisers of production. The Party relies on them, on their experience, skill and knowledge, and looks to them to make the Five-Year Plan a sweeping success.

In mobilising the efforts of this great army of labour the Party, as always, will lean on the trade unions, who are its reliable helpmate in working with the people, in working for the cause of communism.

Comrades, it is almost a year since the 24th CPSU Congress, time to ask ourselves what progress has been made in the implementation of its programme for the country's economic development.

All of you are familiar with the results achieved in the Soviet economy during the year just past. With respect to the main, general figures, such as the growth of national income, industrial output, trade and freight turnover, the results may be assessed as fairly successful. The plan was fulfilled, and in some respects it was overfulfilled. The situation has been somewhat more complicated in agriculture. Owing to poor weather conditions, the results in agriculture were not as successful as had been hoped for. Nevertheless, allowing for the unfavourable objective circumstances, the results may be considered good enough.

All these positive results must be appreciated. In evaluating them the Party has every reason to say to all Soviet working people: We thank you heartily, dear comrades, for your devoted effort, for the great contribution you have made in the past year to the economic progress of our Motherland.

At the same time, as we analyse the results of the first year after the Congress, we should not confine ourselves only to the overall figures. We must dig deeper and see how things stand with respect to the overall improvement of the standard of economic activity, how the qualitative change that the Congress demanded of us is being accomplished. If we approach the results of the economic year from this angle, we shall find a number of problems which merit particular attention.

The situation in the important sphere of capital construction is improving but slowly. The plan for the completion of projects for 1971 was not fulfilled. Periods of construction are still too long. The proportion of so-called "near-complete" projects was even larger than in 1970.

Nor can we be quite satisfied with the results of the year with respect to the introduction of new machinery and the growth of labour efficiency standards. The share of the increment of output due to higher efficiency was short of the plan targets both in industry and in construction, especially in the latter.

The quality of some finished goods improved at a slow rate. This also refers to consumer goods. As a result, quantities of mass consumption goods, such as footwear, clothing and knitwear, pile up at warehouses.

In a word, comrades, in considering the results of the past year we should not take note only of the advances made. The Congress Directives on improving the entire economic activity must be carried out more rapidly and energetically than has been the case until now.

The present Five-Year Plan has been drawn up with regard to the fact that each of us will work better today and tomorrow than he worked yesterday. Let us be frank—this is an indispensable condition for the successful implementation of the Five-Year Plan. If we do not learn how to work better, we may find the plan strenuous indeed. But if we do, we shall accomplish even more than the plan envisages, we shall be able to create a reserve to ensure even more rapid advance in future. A more exacting attitude, a higher sense of responsibility, and unslackening, conscientious work are an earnest of successful fulfilment of all our plans.

It is especially relevant to recall this now in connection with the unusually severe winter of 1972 which made itself felt both in industry and agriculture. Naturally, to overcome the difficulties that have arisen will require considerable effort of Party, government and economic personnel. Much will have to be done in this matter by the trade unions as well. I should like to express confidence that the working people of our country will cope successfully with all the tasks set down in the 1972 economic plan.

Comrades, we are going through an extraordinarily interesting and at the same time highly intricate stage of development. The advance of our economy, the scientific and technological revolution, and changing international conditions make new and greater demands on the style, the methods and the organisation of our entire work.

Thorough reorganisation and improvement of our economic activities, as well as of our work in other fields, as demanded by the 24th Congress, have already started. There is still much to do, however, in the way of searching for new solutions and trying out new methods.

We must all be prepared to adopt this creative style of work. During the next few years we shall have to work out and put into practice measures to implement the course of the economic policy endorsed by the Congress. We mean, first of all, measures for speeding up the progress of science and technology. Considering this to be a question of paramount importance, the CPSU Central Committee has decided to discuss it at one of its plenary meetings. A number of measures to improve economic planning and management and to raise its effectiveness are in preparation. Party and economic bodies must continue to concentrate their attention on advancing agriculture. We have been dealing with these problems for some years now, and much has been done already. However, we must all understand that to accomplish the tasks the Party has set before us will take more years of persevering effort.

In a word, comrades, a tremendous amount of creative work is ahead.

It is indispensable both to the successful fulfilment of the current Five-Year Plan and to providing the groundwork for rapid progress in the future. In the immediate future we shall start working out the long-term perspective of the country's economic development as far ahead as 1990. It must rest on the most accurate, scientifically-based calculation, and the most modern methods of economic management and planning, and forms and patterns of organisation and control. This means that we all shall have to work hard in the field of planning.

Therefore it is of especial importance today that we should master advanced methods of work, economic management and control. That must become a basic principle of our style of work as a whole, of our entire approach to the practical tasks being tackled by the Party and the entire Soviet people.

The main tasks of the Party, government, economic and trade-union bodies in the economic sphere are apparently the following:

— to approach every issue from the standpoint of the concrete implementation of the Ninth Five-Year Plan and of the entire economic and social policy elaborated by the 24th Party Congress;

— to ensure the comprehensive substantiation and effectiveness of economic decisions at all levels, to fulfil the tasks laid down economically, with the least outlays and the maximum benefit for society, and resolutely to fight departmental narrowness and parochialism;

— our common task remains, and this should be stressed once again, to be much more demanding and raise the personal responsibility of the workers of all levels for the work assigned to them, for implementing the decisions of the CPSU Central Committee and the Government. We must cut short violations of Party and state discipline and severely censure those guilty of such violations.

Comrades, the problems referred to above have a direct bearing on trade unions.

Our trade unions operate in a society of triumphant socialism, and that is what determines their basic characteristics. In their struggle for the interests of the working people they have gone beyond the confines of the "protective function," since exploiting classes have been long done away with in our country. To be sure, trade unions are called upon today to protect the working people from "departmental overzeal," as Lenin put it, and from bureaucratic excesses which unfortunately we still come across. But their functions are by no means limited to this. One of the basic distinctions of Soviet trade unions is that they take a direct and active part in the development of society, in raising production and increasing its efficiency, and in economic management.

Trade unions have many tested means of exerting their influence on this decisive sphere of social life. Above all, these include the possibilities that the trade unions have for organising socialist emulation production drives.

The Party Central Committee recently adopted an important decision concerning socialist emulation in today's conditions. Its aim consists essentially in bringing the emulation movement into line with the main directions of the Party's economic policy. This means that the emulation movement should encourage the working people not only to produce more, but also to promote higher quality standards and the saving of money, material and labour resources, to ensure the efficient and prompt employment of scientific and technological achievements in production and to raise labour productivity.

Of no small importance in our work is the proper use of material and moral incentives.

Trade unions which have been invested by law with extensive rights in matters of wages, rate setting and payment scales may help considerably, in particular, to increase the role of payment according to work done, which is a major form of material incentive. New possibilities in this direction have opened up now that the production collectives have at their disposal considerable funds derived from the incomes of their enterprises.

I have mentioned this because of the many instances where there has been an indiscriminate approach in the matter of payment for work and the apportioning of the material incentive funds. To be concerned for the welfare of the working people does not mean to be a good uncle for all workers regardless of their contribution to social production. Everywhere wages should be earned, and everyone should be aware that the size of these wages directly depends on his contribution to the production achievements of one's collective.

On this depends, in the final count, the amount of benefits to be derived by the working man. The benefits to be received by the Soviet people from the new Five-Year Plan will not fall from heaven, will not be given as a gift. They will have to be produced with our own hands, and this requires persistent effort and hard work.

While improving material incentives we must also considerably raise the role of moral incentives.

In our country these incentives are widely used, including such high marks of recognition of one's work as the awarding of orders and honorary titles. Such forms of encouraging the best workers and foremost collectives will certainly retain their full significance.

However, moral incentives should not be limited to awards. Also very important is the ability to create at each enterprise and in each collective such an atmosphere and public opinion that all know who are the workers, and how they work, and each is given his due. Every worker must be able to feel sure that his good work and praiseworthy conduct in the collective will be always acknowledged and appreciated and earn him the respect and gratitude of his workmates. By the same token, everyone should know that no tolerance or leniency will be shown to shirkers, loafers, foot-loose workers and bunglers and that nothing will shield them from the anger of their workmates.

The delegates to the Trade Union Congress will no doubt be giving proper attention to this aspect of the matter—the need for considerably enhancing labour discipline, for fostering conscientiousness—a workingman's conscience, if you like, in every employee.

Vladimir Ilyich Lenin directly linked achievements in socialist construction with "*iron* discipline while at work." He included in the essential rules of behaviour for the Soviet man such as: ". . . do not be lazy . . .", and "observe the strictest labour discipline . . ." Lenin regarded any breach of discipline either by workers or by economic executives as intolerable.

It is precisely because trade unions protect the interests of the working people that they should not—must not—shield those who fail to observe socialist discipline. This calls for an exacting proletarian approach. You should make the fullest possible use of your extensive rights and possibilities in this matter.

It is appropriate to recall, comrades, that Lenin's definition of the role of trade unions as a "school of communism" implies above all the fostering of communist consciousness which is to be inseparably linked with the production activity of people, their work for the benefit of society. The keystone of the trade unions' educational work is the inculcation in the mass of the working people of a truly socialist, communist attitude to work and to public property.

Our trade unions have many other possibilities for effectively helping the Party in implementing its economic policy, including such an important aspect as the acceleration of scientific and technological progress. Today special significance attaches to trade-union activity in raising the qualifications of workers, in the dissemination of scientific and technical knowledge, in educating the working people in the fundamentals of economics, and in promoting the innovators' and inventors' movement.

Trade unions should also give more attention to the important matter of the mechanization of labour. The Party Central Committee recently adopted a special decision on this question which is acquiring major significance. The key directives for solving this problem are laid down, and the ministries and economic and Party bodies will now have to implement them in concrete terms. For trade unions this work is directly linked with their function of labour protection and improvement of working conditions.

Comrades, mention has already been made of the contribution made by trade unions towards raising the living standards of the working people, through participation in the effort to boost production. The significance of this activity of trade unions can hardly be overestimated. But trade unions also fulfil important functions which are directly linked with concern for the living and working conditions of Soviet people, for their welfare.

The competence of trade unions covers many questions concerning wages, material incentives and social insurance; the unions have considerable material facilities for organising health-building holidays and cultural opportunities for the working people, sanatorium and health-resort treatment, tourism, physical culture and sports activities. Trade unions also have great possibilities in such important matters as improving the everyday living conditions of working people, for example, public catering and services. All this affects the interests of millions of people.

This aspect of the activity of trade unions has a direct bearing on such an important issue as the use of free time. Marx observed that free time is the measure of public wealth. Yet free time can truly be considered as a public asset only when it is used in the interests of man's all-round advancement, of developing his abilities and, through this, for still further multiplying the material and cultural potentialities of the entire society. Socialism has furnished all necessary conditions for this; it has given the Soviet man enough free time to rest, to raise his educational and cultural level, to build up his health and promote his physical development, to bring up his children and to meet a variety of other interests. But can we say that free time is always used rationally, to one's benefit and to the benefit of society as a whole? Unfortunately we cannot say so.

Not infrequently this time is senselessly wasted, and sometimes it is used to the detriment of the person concerned and of those around him and, in the final count, to the detriment of the common good. Involved here are instances of anti-social behaviour which are still present. We have been taking and will continue to take stern measures along state and administrative lines to eradicate anti-social manifestations. However, a great role in fighting anti-social behaviour belongs to the public, to workers' collectives and hence to trade unions.

A person's behaviour in everyday life is not only his personal concern. Free time is not a time free from responsibility to society.

Comrades, the 15th Congress of Soviet trade unions concludes an important political campaign in the course of which they have reviewed their work and elected their leading bodies. At the relevant meetings, conferences, and congresses many warm words were addressed to the Communist Party of the Soviet Union and its Central Committee. The workers, office employees, collective farmers and scientists who spoke at these gatherings pointed out that the Soviet trade unions are rallied around the Leninist Communist Party, that the Party leadership had always been and would continue to be the source of strength for the Soviet trade unions.

The Communist Party, which guides the work of the trade unions, shows great concern for the improvement of their activities and creates conditions necessary for their successful work. Over the past several years, the Central Committee of the Communist Party initiated laws which considerably extended the rights of trade unions, and especially those of them which immediately concern the interests of the working people. Of particular importance are the "Fundamental Labour Legislation in the USSR and the Union Republics" and "The Rights of Factory and Office Trade Union Committees" adopted by the Supreme Soviet of the USSR.

The Communist Party favours a more active participation of industrial and office workers through trade unions in the management of industrial enterprises. Production conferences and workers' meetings, at which working plans for factories, plants and state farms, social development schemes and other questions are discussed, are an important form of socialist democracy, public control, a form of drawing the working people into the sphere of industrial management.

An essential form of assistance by the Party to trade union organisations must also be its support for the trade unions in their just demands to management, and in ensuring that collective agreements are observed, so that each executive will be aware of his duties and of his obligation to consult trade union organisations and to seek the opinion and advice of industrial and office workers.

From this rostrum I should like to address millions of Communists, trade union members. On you, comrades, on your active work largely depend the general level and effectiveness of

the trade union organisations of which you are members. The
Party requires every Communist who is a trade union member,
not to be a mere member of his trade union organisation, but
also to be an active participant in its work. The Party has laid
down important requirements for Communists elected to trade
union bodies. It teaches them to hold dear the trust put in
them by the people, and to justify this trust with practical
work.

The policy of the Party with regard to the trade unions, as
pointed out at the 24th Congress, is aimed at raising the level
of the entire work of the trade unions. As before, the Party will
exert further efforts to see to it that the trade unions fulfill their
role as a school of economic guidance, a school of economic
management, and a school of communist attitude to work.

Comrades, speaking at this Trade Union Congress, I should
like to dwell now on the part the working class plays in the development of Soviet society.

The Soviet working class of today differs not only from the
pre-revolutionary proletariat but also from the working class
of the 1930's when socialism triumphed in the USSR. Its role as
the leading socio-political and economic force of society has
grown. It is now the largest class in our country. In the years of
Soviet rule the working class has grown six times to a total of
65 million people, with more than two-thirds of this number
being industrial workers. The level of their education and industrial skill has risen immeasurably. Suffice it to say that
since 1939 the number of workers with a full secondary education—both specialised and general—has grown by more than 30
times. The working class now plays a tremendous role not only
in industry but also in farm production. The number of workers employed in the agrarian sector of our economy totals nine
million. This number will grow in the future as the nature of
agricultural work comes increasingly to approximate industrial
work.

The advanced worker of today is a man equipped with
knowledge, a man of culture, who has a conscientious and creative attitude to his work, who feels himself to be the master of

production; a man who is responsible for everything that takes place in our society. Such a worker is a politically active person, he is intolerant of acts of irresponsibility, of a sloppy attitude to work, of any shortcomings in the organisation of the production process. He is the irreconcilable enemy of all manifestations of philistinism, of all survivals of the past in the consciousness and behaviour of people.

The ideals of the Party, the ideals of communism have become for such a worker the essence of his entire outlook. They are at the root of all his actions, his attitude to people and his whole life.

It is very important to instil these qualities in the younger generation of our working class. The school, the Young Communist League and trade unions must organise their work in such a way that every young man and woman will be aware of the role and the grandeur of the man of labour, the historical mission of the working class, and will want to join its glorious ranks.

At the present stage of communist construction the alliance of the working class, collective farmers and the working intellectuals of our country is assuming ever greater importance. The working class which plays, and will continue to play the leading role in the building of a communist society, remains the cementing force of this great alliance. It is on this basis that the ideological, political and social consolidation of Soviet society, and the drawing closer together of all the nations and nationalities of our country are taking place.

One of the guiding principles of our life is proletarian internationalism, which is inseparable from the position of the working class in our society.

The working class of our country has always regarded the cause for which it is fighting as part of the international struggle of the proletariat of all countries. From the very beginning the working class has acted as an international force. To honour the principles of internationalism, to do its lofty duty by its own people and the working people of the world, as history has elected it to do, the working class of our country has made many sacrifices, performed great feats of heroism and displayed firmness of spirit and will.

The Soviet working class has rendered universally recognised services to the world revolutionary movement. It is true that in the class struggle in the world arena—the fight against imperialism and the struggle for the freedom of nations and for socialism—its role is different from that of the working class of capitalist countries. Nevertheless, its role in this struggle is great, for it is with the hands, brains and energy of the working class, of all working men and women of the Soviet Union and other socialist countries, that the economic might and defence potential of socialism, which play the primary role in the consolidation of peace and in the struggle for the social progress of mankind, have been created.

The force of example, which socialism provides, has always played an important role in the development of the international working class movement. There is no denying the fact that the achievements of the Soviet Union in the field of social security and protection of the rights of the working people have become an inspiring example for workers in other countries, and in their class struggle against exploitation and capitalist oppression.

At the present stage, the force of our example in the sphere of production and scientific and technical progress has assumed special importance, and in this the Soviet working class, together with our scientists and engineers, is called upon to play the foremost role, for it works in the conditions of an advanced and mature socialist society, and is engaged in creating the material and technical base of communism. It is understandable why the Soviet working class is held up as an example to the world of what the working man can achieve under socialism, and of what possibilities the socialist system has. This is a mark of honour; it also means a great historical responsibility.

Thus, on the productive, political and social activity of the Soviet workers and of the working class of other socialist countries largely depend the might of the "world-wide, great army of labour" and the speed at which it forges ahead towards socialism.

The ranks of the international working class—the most advanced revolutionary class of our time, and its role as the main productive and socio-political force in the world will continue to grow. Despite fashionable anti-Marxist theories which hold that the scientific and technological revolution is limiting the scope of activities of the working class and will eventually lead to its liquidation, facts speak to the contrary: scientific and technical progress everywhere leads to the growth of the working class, for among other things it creates new occupations.

The capitalist world is being shaken by a tremendous upsurge of the working class movement. In a number of countries this upsurge has become an important factor of socio-political life. The class battles which are unfolding today have given rise to a tendency to which the Communists have called attention, namely the gradual turning of the economic struggle into actions directed against the entire system of state-monopoly domination. Evidence of this is the recent successful strike of the British coal miners, the great strike actions of the Italian workers, and the large-scale strikes in a number of other countries. We hail the successes of the working class movement in Latin America, Asia and Africa.

Our Communist Party, workers, all Soviet working people voice their solidarity with the struggle of our class brothers. And we convey to them our militant proletarian greetings. The growing cohesion and trade-union unity of the working people of the capitalist countries, the determination with which they are fighting to secure their demands, and the proletarian firmness with which they defend their rights and uphold their class dignity have our admiration.

Our Party has attached great significance to the international ties between trade unions, especially since this involves direct participation of the Soviet people in the world working class movement, in the strengthening of cohesion and business-like cooperation among the working people of the socialist countries, and in their struggle for peace and social progress.

Permit me to greet, through the representatives of foreign trade unions, all the sections of the world working class and trade union movement.

The Communist Parties have always been in the van of the class struggle of the working people. Permit me, on behalf of our Party, the Soviet working class, all working people of our country, to convey from this rostrum our feelings of internationalist solidarity to the fraternal parties, and to wish them further success in their struggle.

Comrade delegates,

Questions of foreign policy constitute an integral and essential part of the activities of our Party and State.

The principal objectives and tasks of our foreign policy at the current stage have been mapped out by the 24th Congress of the CPSU. The Programme endorsed by the Congress, which has come to be known as the Soviet peace programme, is being consistently implemented and has become an important factor in world politics.

Our principled course constitutes an active defence of peace, freedom and the security of nations. We pursue it together with our friends and allies, coordinating our steps in the international arena. The countries of the socialist community have a common coordinated policy on practically all basic questions of world politics. Experience has shown this to be of invaluable importance for the successful conduct of our foreign policy matters.

As you know, comrades, the meeting of the Political Consultative Committee of the Warsaw Treaty Member-States held in Prague in January concentrated on the European problems.

Resolutions were adopted whose essential aim is to promote European security, give concrete embodiment to the idea of cooperation among the European states, and help settle the outstanding European problems.

Europe is on the threshold of a new stage of development. The ideas of peace, security, and the development of comprehensive cooperation are being accepted and supported by a growing number of states. Peace initiatives of the socialist countries have helped create a situation which makes it possible to tackle the problems of security and cooperation in Europe. The solution of these problems is a task of historic magnitude. The European working class and its trade unions are called upon to play an important role in this matter. As you know, we have proposed the convocation of an all-European conference in the interests of European security.

It seems that there is not a single state in Europe that has not come out, in one way or another, in support of the conference on security and cooperation. Canada has voiced support of this proposal. As it follows from what President Nixon told the Congress, the USA too supports the idea of such a conference. We should now settle the question of when the contemplated conference is to be held and jointly formulate the main lines of its work.

The socialist countries have set forth their proposals on this matter in their Declaration of Peace, Security and Cooperation in Europe adopted at the meeting of the Political Consultative Committee of the Warsaw Treaty Member-States, held in Prague.

The socialist countries consistently promote the development of mutually advantageous relations with the capitalist states of Europe. And notable results have been achieved in this field. This is particularly true of our relations with France, Finland and the Scandinavian countries.

Considerable progress has been made in our relations with the Federal Republic of Germany. This has been made possible by the signing of the Treaties between the USSR and the FRG and between Poland and the FRG.

These Treaties are now in the process of being ratified. Debates on the matter are being held in the USSR Supreme Soviet, in the Seim of the Polish People's Republic, and in the legislative bodies of the FRG.

Undoubtedly, the ratification of the Treaty between the USSR and the FRG will usher in an essentially new and more fruitful stage of development of Soviet-West German relations in various fields. This, we believe, would be in the best interests of the USSR and the FRG and it would be of utmost importance for European peace.

The question of the ratification of the Treaties has given rise to a sharp struggle in the Federal Republic of Germany. Some politicians oppose the Treaties and even attempt to cast doubt on the very possibility of a real reconciliation and development of normal relations between the FRG and the socialist countries.

What do the opponents of the Treaties want? They make no secret of their plans. They hold that the Treaties are bad because they formalize the inviolability of the European borders, and they talk of "revising" the Articles of the Treaties that bear on this subject. But is it not clear that the opponents of the Treaties will never find partners in talks to revise the borders? This is no matter for discussion either now or in the future. The borders of the socialist countries are inviolable and here the Treaties simply reflect reality.

The opponents of the Treaty do not hide the fact that they wish to weaken the sovereignty of the German Democratic Republic. Here, too, they would like to return to the past. The German Democratic Republic has been steadily advancing along the socialist path for almost 25 years now. It takes an active part in international life. Those who shut their eyes to this and could not draw the proper conclusions are only capable of driving their policies into a blind alley. It is high time they realised that the situation in Europe cannot be normalized without taking into full account the position of the GDR as an independent and sovereign socialist country.

The FRG now faces a crucial choice which will determine the destinies of its people and the attitude to it of other countries for years ahead. This is a choice between cooperation and confrontation, between a detente and the aggravation of tensions, and, finally, this is a choice between a policy of peace and a policy of war.

As for the Soviet Union, we are sincere and earnest in our approach to the question of improving our relations with the FRG, although for obvious reasons this is no simple question for our country. The hardships of the past war and suffering which Hitlerite aggression inflicted on our people are still alive in the memory of the Soviet people. But we believe that the grim past should not forever remain an insuperable obstacle to the development of our relations with West Germany. We also take account of the fact that the bulk of the West German population are for improvement of relations with the Soviet Union and the other socialist countries.

Comrades, in the vast and manifold activities now being carried on by the Governments and the public of many countries to lay the foundations of a lasting peace in Europe the resistance of certain forces in the West which do not want a detente in Europe and do their utmost to prevent it has to be overcome. Precisely these forces are trying to complicate the preparation of an all-European conference; they think up various pretexts to delay its convocation. They are trying to spread the absurd idea that the proposal to hold the conference and our European policy in general aim to torpedo the European Economic Community or the Common Market as it is usually called. It is apparently necessary to say a few words on this matter.

The Soviet Union does not at all ignore the situation that has taken shape in Western Europe, nor does it disregard the existence of such an economic grouping of capitalist states as the Common Market. We closely follow the activities of the Common Market and its evolution. Our relations with the members of this grouping will naturally depend on the extent to which they, for their part, will recognize the realities that have shaped up in the socialist part of Europe and, in particular, the interests of the countries belonging to the Council for Mutual Economic Assistance. We stand for equality in economic relations and we are against discrimination.

Comrades, the principal objective of Soviet foreign policy is elimination of the hot-beds of wars and rebuff of imperialist encroachments on the freedom and independence of nations.

The war in Indochina which, by the admission of the US President, is the longest and hardest war in American history, has shown the utter untenability of the imperialist policy of aggression and oppression of nations. The USA now counts above all on local mercenaries in its attempts to strangle the national liberation struggle in Indochina in order to retain its political and strategic positions in this area. This is what Washington calls "Vietnamization" of the war. It wants to replace US uniform tattered by the Indochinese patriots by the uniform of puppet soldiery, but the political lining remains the same—American.

The patriots of Vietnam, Laos and Cambodia see through these manoeuvres. With the assistance and support of the Soviet Union and the other socialist countries, the peoples of Indochina are carrying on their struggle against the aggressor on the military, diplomatic and political fronts.

In the struggle the Soviet people are entirely on the side of the peoples of Indochina. It is our internationalist duty to help them and we shall fulfil it unfailingly. The Soviet Union resolutely condemns the piratical bombings of the territory of the Democratic Republic of Vietnam by the US Air Force and demands that they be stopped. We fully support the just proposals of the DRV and the Republic of South Vietnam. We demand that the invaders withdraw from Indochina; we demand independence for the peoples of this region and hold that they should be able to determine their destinies without any outside interference and pressure.

The danger implicit in the tense situation in the Middle East is increasing. The stubborn refusal by Israel to withdraw from the Arab lands she has seized and the incessant provocations by the Israeli military against the Arab states exacerbate the situation threatening an outbreak of hostilities.

The Arab countries have convincingly demonstrated their readiness to reach a political settlement of the conflict and to establish a stable and durable peace in the Middle East. Israel, aided and abetted by the USA, stubbornly clings to its aggressive policy of annexation. This, however, cannot continue forever. Sober-minded politicians cannot expect that the Arab states will tolerate the occupation of their territories.

The Arab world today is not what it used to be several years ago. The progressive regimes have been consolidated; cooperation between the Arab states is being promoted, and the defence capacity of the Arab states has been greatly strengthened. All these are long-term factors, and, in the final count, they will determine the correlation of forces in the Middle East.

Friendship and cooperation between the Soviet Union and the progressive Arab states are being steadily promoted; cooperation in matters of economy and defence is being furthered, and political coordination is being enhanced. It can be said that our relations with our Arab friends have never been as firmly based and all-pervading as now. We shall continue to strengthen and develop these relations in the best interests of our countries, in the name of justice, freedom and progress of the Arab peoples, for the sake of a lasting peace in the Middle East.

Comrades, you have probably noticed that questions pertaining to Asian countries have lately become prominent in our policies. This is quite understandable. Nearly two-thirds of Soviet territory are situated on the Asian continent. And owing to the success of the fight for national and social emancipation and economic advance by the Asian peoples, Asia's role in world politics is growing rapidly.

The Soviet Union has always favoured and continues to favour development of the best of relations with Asian states. Our goal is to promote peace in Asia and to help its progressive forces fight imperialism and colonialism in every form.

We maintain and are successfully developing fraternal relations and all-round cooperation with the socialist countries in Asia, such as the Mongolian People's Republic, the Democratic Republic of Vietnam and the Korean People's Democratic Republic.

We are happy to note that good relations have developed between our country and many Asian countries, particularly, Afghanistan, Burma, Ceylon, Iran and Turkey, although our relations with some of these countries could have been better than they are at the present time. For our part we shall do our utmost to promote these relations.

We attach especially great importance to our growing friendship with India and her great people that are traversing a road of freedom, independence and progress. Our relations with India have never stopped developing over the entire period of her existence as an independent state. Of this development the Soviet-Indian Agreement on Peace, Friendship and Cooperation was born.

In our wish to consolidate our friendship with India we have met with complete understanding on the part of the Indian Government headed by Indira Gandhi, the outstanding leader of the people of India.

As you know, a new situation has now taken shape on the Indian subcontinent. The liberation struggle of the people of East Bengal has brought forth a new independent state, the People's Republic of Bangladesh. Seventy-five million people have won their right to independence and national advancement, and we have sincerely congratulated them on their great victory.

Our policy of support for, and cooperation with, the Republic of Bangladesh is based on the general foreign policy principles followed by the Communist Party and the Soviet State. Prime Minister Shaikh Mujibur Rahman of Bangladesh visited the Soviet Union recently. It is our hope that this visit will become an important landmark in the relations between our countries. For our part we shall continue in future, too, to do everything in our power to promote the development and consolidation of our relations with the Republic of Bangladesh.

I would like to emphasize, however, that we are also for establishing good relations with Pakistan; there are no conflicts, no controversies, that separate our two countries. The visit to the Soviet Union of President Bhutto of Pakistan that ended a few days ago shows that there are essential prerequisites for the development of good relations between our countries.

We are also consistent advocates of the establishment of a

stable peace and good-neighbourly relations among India, Pakistan and Bangladesh. To achieve this would mean to make an important contribution to improving the political atmosphere throughout Asia.

Of late a turn for the better has been observed in our relations with Japan. Not long ago the Soviet Union and Japan reached an agreement on holding talks to conclude a peace treaty. We consider this an important, positive development. We are confident that complete normalization of Soviet-Japanese relations would fully accord not only with the interests of our two peoples, but also with the general interests of peace and security in the Far East and in the Pacific Basin. As for us, we are ready to establish and develop large-scale mutually advantageous cooperation with Japan both in the economic and the political spheres, bearing it in mind that such cooperation will serve the cause of peace.

The idea of ensuring Asian security on a collective basis has aroused growing interest in many Asian countries. It is becoming increasingly clear that the road to security in Asia is not one of military blocs and groupings, not one of opposing the countries against each other, but one of good-neighbourly cooperation among all the states interested in such cooperation.

To our mind, collective security in Asia should be based on such principles as renunciation of the use of force in relations between states, respect for sovereignty and inviolability of borders, non-interference in domestic affairs and extensive development of economic and other cooperation on the basis of complete equality and mutual advantage. We have advocated the establishment of such collective security in Asia and will continue to do so; we are ready to cooperate with all countries for the sake of carrying out this idea.

Not long ago the visit to China of President Nixon of the United States and his talks with the Peking leaders attracted much public attention. What do we have to say on this subject?

First of all, the restoration of contacts between two states and normalization of relations between them is quite natural. The Soviet Union has always been against the imperialist policy of isolation of the People's Republic of China; it has always favoured due recognition of China's role on the international scene. However, an assessment of the current contacts between Peking and Washington should take into account the basis of these contacts.

The parties to the Peking meetings have said little about what they discussed and what they agreed on to the peoples, to the world at large. Indeed, they made it clear that they would keep secret and "not discuss" that which lay outside the limits of the official communique. Thus, facts and future actions of the United States and the People's Republic of China will reveal the true significance of the Peking talks.

However, one must not overlook certain statements by the parties to the Peking talks which give us grounds to believe that the dialogue went beyond the framework of bilateral relations between the USA and China. How else is one to understand, for instance, the statement made during the banquet in Shanghai that "today our two peoples [i.e. American and Chinese] hold the future of the whole world in their hands"?

It is a well-known fact that even quite recently the policy of peaceful coexistence, which the Soviet Union has consistently followed since the time of Lenin, was referred to in Peking as "revisionism" and "betrayal of the revolution." Now the principles of peaceful coexistence have been confirmed in the Sino-American communique. This is certainly to be welcomed. But it is important not just to lay down these principles on paper, but also to implement them.

In general, it should be noted that there are various views and guesses concerning the Peking meeting. But views aside, I repeat that the decisive word remains to be spoken by facts and actions. This is why we do not hurry to make our final assessment. The future, probably the near future, will show how things really stand, and then it will be time for us to draw the appropriate conclusions.

As far as our relations with the People's Republic of China are concerned, the principled position of our Party and the Soviet State was clearly outlined in the documents of the 24th Congress of the CPSU. The Congress resolution points out that our Party adheres to the position of consistent defence of the principles of Marxism-Leninism, all-round consolidation of the unity of the world communist movement and defence of the interests of our socialist Motherland. It goes on to say: "The Congress resolutely rejects the slanderous inventions of Chinese propaganda concerning the policy of our Party and State. At the same time our Party stands for normalization of relations between the USSR and the PRC, and restoration of good-neighbourliness and friendship between the Soviet and Chinese peoples. Improvement of relations between the Soviet Union and the People's Republic of China would meet the vital, long-term interests of both countries, the interests of world socialism, the interests of intensifying the struggle against imperialism." This position remains fully valid today too.

Chinese official representatives tell us that relations between the USSR and the People's Republic of China should be based on the principles of peaceful coexistence. Well, if Peking does not find it possible to go further in its relations with a socialist state, we are prepared to conduct Soviet-Chinese relations on this basis today. I can say, comrades, that we not only proclaim such readiness, but we translate it into the language of concrete and constructive proposals on non-aggression, on settlement of border disputes, on improvement of relations on a mutually advantageous foundation. The Chinese leaders have known these proposals a long time. The next move is China's.

Comrades, each step towards a relaxation of international tension, in the cause of defence of the inalienable rights of the peoples, is accomplished in sharp confrontation with the forces of militarism and reaction.

Apparently some gentlemen intend to add to the dangerous crisis in the Middle East a new source of friction, now in the Mediterranean, for how else is one to understand the agreement between the United States and the present regime in Greece concerning the placing of the Greek port of Piraeus at the disposal of the US Sixth Fleet? How else is one to understand the crude attempts at interference in the internal affairs of Cyprus and the ultimatum demanding the formation of a new government there, all of which is intended actually to liquidate the independence and territorial integrity of the State of Cyprus. The same is meant by NATO's hard pressure on Malta, the youngest state in the Mediterranean.

Together with our friends we vigilantly follow and counteract imperialist intrigues in the region directly abutting on the southern frontiers of the socialist community.

In formulating our foreign and defence policies we cannot ignore the fact that the armaments build-up is continuing in a number of imperialist countries. The new budget which is now being considered in Washington envisages a considerable rise in military spending, particularly on long-term strategic armaments programmes. The United States demands greater military allocations from its NATO allies, as well.

Calm and vigilant, the Soviet Union is following a resolute anti-imperialist policy, and consistently and firmly defending the interests of socialism, the freedom of the peoples and the cause of universal peace. The struggle for disarmament is an important component of this policy.

The disarmament proposals put forward by the 24th CPSU Congress have already demonstrated their validity.

Our initiative in calling a world disarmament conference has met with a broad and favourable international response. In a special resolution the UN General Assembly has approved this idea and decided to continue to examine the possibilities of convening a world conference.

On the initiative of the socialist countries a convention has been worked out banning bacteriological weapons and envisaging the complete elimination of their stockpiles. The convention is expected to be endorsed soon.

We regard as useful the Soviet-American agreement reached

last autumn on reducing the danger of a nuclear war. The Soviet Union would like the other nuclear powers to be party to the agreement in some form.

We attach great importance to the Soviet-American talks on limiting strategic armaments. The key to their success would be the recognition by the two parties of the principle of equal security of the sides and readiness to abide by this principle in practice. We are for reaching a mutually acceptable agreement. Such agreement would meet the interests of both the Soviet and the American peoples, and the interests of international security.

In Soviet foreign policy vigorous rebuff to the aggressive ventures of imperialism is combined with constructive approach to international issues ripe for settlement, and irreconcilability in ideological struggle with readiness to develop mutually advantageous relations with the states of the opposing social system. The coming talks in Moscow with President Nixon of the United States may occupy a prominent place among the visits and meetings which we undertake for the sake of developing such relations. As is known, these talks are due to open on May 22.

Our approach to the coming Soviet-American talks is businesslike and realistic. We are well aware of the significance the state of Soviet-American relations has for the future of the peoples of these two countries, and for the international situation as a whole, for the question whether this situation will develop in the direction of a stable peace, or mounting tensions.

Thus, we consider it useful to extend such spheres in the relations between the USSR and the USA that would permit us, without renouncing the principles of our policy, to achieve mutually advantageous cooperation in the interests of the peoples of the two countries, and of consolidating world peace.

We have said before and we affirm now that improvement of relations between the USSR and the USA is possible. Moreover, it is desirable, but, naturally, not at the expense of third countries or peoples, not at the expense of their legitimate rights and interests. Such is our firm stand.

\* \* \*

Comrades, each successive stage in the building of communism puts before the Soviet people and its communist vanguard tasks of increasing complexity and scope, requiring of them a still greater sense of responsibility, still wider knowledge and political activity.

The Soviet trade unions have come to their 15th Congress as a respected, strong and influential force of Soviet society, steeled in the struggle for socialism. The trade unions have proved by their activities that they were, are and will be a reliable support of the Party, the respected and competent organisers of the people engaged in building communism.

This year the Soviet people will celebrate an important date—the 50th anniversary of the formation of the Union of Soviet Socialist Republics. The Party calls on the working class, collective farmers, intellectuals, all Soviet working people to mark the anniversary of this great historic event by taking an energetic part in the socialist emulation drive, by achieving new records in their work.

I am happy to inform you, comrade delegates, that the Presidium of the USSR Supreme Soviet, in recognition of the great contribution of the Soviet trade unions to the building of socialism and communism and to the achievement of the targets of economic development plans, has awarded the trade unions of the Union of Soviet Socialist Republics the Order of Lenin.

This means that the highest award in the Soviet Union has been conferred on the working class, the intellectuals and the large army of agricultural workers for their services to their country in the 8th Five-Year Plan period. And in informing you of the decoration of the trade unions with the Order of Lenin, I should like to quote the words with which Lenin concluded his letter to the 5th All-Russia Congress of Trade Unions, the last in his lifetime: "To make every effort to intensify and improve our work in all fields . . ."

The Central Committee is convinced that this high award of our Motherland will encourage the Soviet trade unions to perform new feats for the sake of carrying out the great plans of communist construction, charted by the 24th Congress of the Communist Party of the Soviet Union.

Allow me to give to the Presidium the letter of greetings from the Central Committee of the Party to the 15th Congress of the Trade Unions of the USSR.

# Part VII

## THE 50TH ANNIVERSARY OF THE
## UNION OF SOVIET SOCIALIST REPUBLICS

Dear Comrades,

Dear Foreign Guests,

These days, the chimes of the Spassky Tower of the Kremlin have an especially stirring ring for the Soviet people. We are approaching the moment when the main timepiece of the Soviet Union will strike the hour marking fifty years since the day the Union of Soviet Socialist Republics was formed. We have met here today in this ceremonial atmosphere together with our esteemed foreign guests to celebrate the glorious jubilee of our multinational federal state.

The formation of the USSR was a direct continuation of the cause of the Great October Revolution, which opened up a new era in mankind's development; it was a practical embodiment of the idea of our great leader, Lenin—the idea of a voluntary union of free nations.

The half-century history of the Union of Soviet Socialist Republics is that of the emergence of the indissoluble unity and friendship of all the nations united within the framework of the Soviet socialist state. It is the history of the unprecedented growth and all-round development of the state which was born of the socialist revolution and which is now one of the mightiest powers in the world. It is the history of the growth to maturity of all the Republics that have united under the banner of the Soviet state, of all the nations, big and small, which inhabit the country, and their attainment of true prosperity—economic, political and cultural.

Dear Compatriots,

Comrades,

On the occasion of this historic jubilee of the USSR we address words of profound respect and gratitude to the millions upon millions of Soviet people of every generation. We address those who created and built the great Soviet Union with revolutionary courage and dedicated labour, those who heroically defended its freedom, independence and honour in its hour of danger in the hardest-fought war in history, and those who have carried the Soviet Union to its present powerful, glorious and thriving state, and who are now blazing the trail for all mankind into the communist future.

We have feelings of the most profound respect and gratitude to all those who are totally dedicated to the Leninist union of free nations, to those whose labour and enthusiasm are making our beloved country stronger and more beautiful every day—we mean the great working class and the working people on the collective farms, our intelligentsia, our valorous men of the Soviet Army, our wonderful women. We address greetings to our young people, who are taking over from the older generations in a fitting manner and on whom largely depends what the Union of Soviet Socialist Republics will be like as it enters the third millennium of our era.

Dear comrades, to all of you we extend our congratulations on this great celebration!

Congratulations to all of you on the golden jubilee of our federal socialist multinational state!

# I.

# THE FORMATION OF THE
# USSR—A TRIUMPH OF THE
# LENINIST NATIONAL POLICY

Comrades, in these anniversary holidays one's mind, quite naturally, goes back to that distant time in December 1922 when the First All-Union Congress of Soviets adopted its Declaration and Treaty on the Formation of the Union of Soviet Socialist Republics. The more one ponders historical facts, the more clearly does one see the wisdom of the Leninist Party, which consolidated the success of the October Revolution and the subsequent radical social changes by establishing the unbreakable union of equal Soviet Republics.

The struggle against the enemies of the Revolution and for the victory of socialism in our country required the closest unity of the peoples that had flung off the yoke of tsarism, the bourgeoisie and the landowners. The collapse of the old world, the break-up of the exploitative system, the establishment of the dictatorship of the proletariat and the consolidation of social property in the means of production went hand in hand with fierce class struggle, which developed into a civil war. The young Soviet country was savagely attacked by the forces of internal counter-revolution and world imperialism.

The working class confronted the united counter-revolution with the great strength of proletarian solidarity born of the

Revolution. The sons of all the peoples of our country fought shoulder to shoulder under the revolutionary banners of the Red Army in the central areas of the country, in the steppes of the Ukraine and the Volga Area, on the Don and the Kuban, by the White Sea and in the mountains of the Caucasus, in the sands of Central Asia and in the distant Amur territory. Together they went into battle for peace, bread and land, for the power of the Soviets. During the years of the Civil War, as in the unforgettable days of the Great October Revolution, the internationalist solidarity of the working class and of all the working people was one of the vital sources of our victory. In those early years after the October Revolution all the Soviet Republics then in existence had already formed a close political, military, economic and diplomatic alliance formalised in a number of treaties.

The Civil War and the defeat of the enemies of the Revolution was followed by a period of peaceful construction. Each Soviet Republic naturally faced these questions: What was the next step? What forms of statehood were to be chosen? How were relations with the fraternal Republics to be built?

For the mass of working people the experience of the three revolutions in Russia, the Bolshevik Party's internationalist slogans, the Decrees on Peace and on Land, the policy of the Communists and Lenin's very name became a symbol of joint struggle for a new life. The working class and the working people of all nationalities wished to strengthen their unity, which had already borne such important fruit in the earlier period.

In order to advance along the path of building socialism, all the Soviet Republics had first to cope with the dislocation, to rehabilitate the productive forces undermined by the wars, to overcome their backwardness and to improve the working people's living standards. These tasks could best and soonest be carried out by developing the economies under a common plan, and making rational use of the potentialities for division of labour among the various parts of the country.

Finally, there was the continued threat of fresh imperialist intervention. It would have been hard to safeguard Soviet power and the independence of the country surrounded as it was by militarily strong capitalist powers, without the closest union, without uniting to the fullest extent the fraternal Republics' military, political and diplomatic efforts.

Thus, the vital interests of all the Soviet peoples, and the very logic of the struggle for socialism in this country demanded the formation of a united multinational socialist state. But the establishment of such a state required the Party's organising role, correct policy and purposeful activity.

Indeed, the Communist Party did have the necessary theoretical basis for such a policy—the Marxist-Leninist doctrine on the national question. This doctrine constituted an important component part of the theory of socialist revolution.

Communists have always viewed the national question through the prism of the class struggle, believing that its solution had to be subordinated to the interests of the Revolution, to the interests of socialism. That is why Communists and all fighters for socialism believe that the main aspect of the national question is unification of the working people, regardless of their national origin, in the common battle against every type of oppression, and for a new social system which rules out exploitation of the working people.

Lenin spoke of this with the utmost clarity: "We are consistent internationalists and are striving for the voluntary alliance of the workers and peasants of all nations."

But what was the basis for establishing such an alliance? Lenin was deeply convinced that it could be established only on the basis of complete equality and mutual respect of all its participants. "We want a *voluntary* union of nations," he emphasised, "a union which precludes any coercion of one nation by another—a union founded on complete confidence, on a clear awareness of brotherly unity, on absolutely voluntary consent."

Thus, the unity of the working people of all nations is one of the basic prerequisites for the triumph of the Revolution. On the other hand, only the triumph of the socialist revolution can ensure the full triumph of the cause of national liberation.

This was quite clearly stated by Karl Marx and Frederick Engels in the Communist Manifesto: "In proportion as the antagonism between classes within the nation vanishes, the hostility of one nation to another will come to an end."

Such is the dialectics of the Marxist-Leninist approach to the national question: the way to cohesion, unity and the all-round integration of nations lies through their complete liberation from social and national oppression, through the creation of the most favourable conditions for the development of each nation.

The national question was an especially acute one in Russia because of her specific conditions. The exploiting classes of tsarist Russia deliberately spread national strife and hostility, acting on the "divide and rule" principle which oppressors have practised in every epoch. Although tsarist Russia was one of the major powers at the time, she herself was subjected to imperialist plunder. Accordingly, the Land of Soviets was faced, on the one hand, with the problem of creating fundamentally new relations between the nations and nationalities within the country—relations of trust, friendship, and fraternal cooperation—and on the other, the problem of defending and ensuring the national independence of the young Soviet state in international relations.

It was up to our Party to do what even the most advanced capitalist states which boast of their democracy have always been unable to do. It is, after all, a fact that even today the nationalities question remains highly acute in the USA, Canada, and Belgium, to say nothing of Great Britain, where English imperialism has for many years been carrying on a savage war against the people of Northern Ireland, who have risen to struggle for their rights.

Literally within a week after the birth of the Soviet state its famous Declaration of the Rights of the Peoples of Russia put on record these principles of the national policy of the Soviet Government: the equality and sovereignty of the peoples of Russia; the right of nations to free self-determination, including secession and the establishment of an independent state;

the abolition of all manner of national and national-religious privileges and restrictions; the free development of the national minorities; the need for a voluntary and honest alliance of the peoples of Russia and their complete mutual trust.

In the early years after the October Revolution, the Party, headed by Lenin, put in a great effort in explaining to the working masses its policy in the sphere of national-state construction. Among those who took an active part in this work were the prominent Party leaders—M. I. Kalinin and F. E. Dzerzhinsky, Y. M. Sverdlov and J. V. Stalin, S. M. Kirov and G. K. Ordzhonikidze, M. V. Frunze and S. G. Shaumyan, G. I. Petrovsky and A. G. Chervyakov, N. Narimanov and A. T. Dzhangildin, P. I. Stucka and M. G. Tskhakaya, and many other comrades.

The Party put its revolutionary energy, its great effort and determination into the historic endeavour of creating a socialist multinational state. The Tenth Congress of the RCP(B) noted that the establishment of the Soviet system and the measures carried out by the Party ". . . transformed relations between the toiling masses of the nationalities of Russia, overcame the old national hostility, destroyed the basis of national oppression, and won for the Russian workers the trust of their brother workers of other nationalities not only in Russia but also in Europe and Asia, and raised this trust to enthusiasm and a readiness to fight for the common cause . . ."

The Party's work among the masses, the experience of national construction already gained by the RSFSR, the Ukraine, Byelorussia, the Transcaucasian Federation and the Autonomous Republics, and the powerful movement for unification which started in all the Republics—all of this paved the way for the establishment of a united socialist state.

It was necessary, however, to find forms of a union state, and to balance the powers of the all-Union bodies and of the Republics in a way that would best ensure unity.

During the discussion of these questions, which began in the autumn of 1922, different tendencies emerged. Some believed that it was possible merely to establish some sort of confederation of the Republics, without setting up common federative bodies vested with extensive powers. Others proposed "autonomisation," that is, the entry of all the fraternal Republics into the RSFSR on an autonomous basis. It took Lenin's genius to overcome these erroneous tendencies and to find the only right way.

Lenin put forward the plan of establishing one federal state in the form of a voluntary union of equal Republics. The power of the Soviets, which had sprung from the Revolution and which had already proved viable in practice, was the natural basis for such a federal state. On October 6, 1922, a plenary meeting of the RCP(B) Central Committee supported Lenin's initiative and deemed it necessary "to conclude a treaty between the Ukraine, Byelorussia, the Federation of the Transcaucasian Republics, and the RSFSR on their unification into a Union of Socialist Soviet Republics."

The First All-Union Congress of Soviets opened in Moscow on December 30 and, in response to the proposals put forward by the congresses of Soviets in the Ukraine, Byelorussia, Transcaucasia and the RSFSR, adopted its historic decision setting up the world's first multinational socialist state—the Union of Soviet Socialist Republics.

This event was a fitting outcome of the first five years of Soviet government, the workers' and peasants' power. The power born of the Revolution not only withstood all the storms, calamities and dangers but also united the working people of our multinational country into the mighty and solid Soviet Union!

That same day, December 30, 1922, the fine city of Moscow was named the capital of the Soviet Union.

In short, December 30, 1922, is a truly historic date in the life of our state, an important milestone in the life of all the Soviet peoples, their great festival. We have a Constitution Day. It would perhaps be a good idea subsequently to combine these two holidays and to mark December 30 as the Day of the Formation of the USSR. This will be a day of friendship and brotherhood of our peoples, a festival of socialist internationalism!

Comrades, the formation of the Soviet Union and the subsequent formation and entry into it of new Union Republics have multiplied the forces and potentialities of the peoples of our country in socialist construction. The Union of Soviet Socialist Republics, a great socialist power, has come to occupy a fitting place in the world arena with great benefit for the cause of peace, freedom and independence of all the nations of the globe.

When closing the Tenth All-Russia Congress of Soviets, M. I. Kalinin said: ". . . Do we not cherish the name of the RSFSR? We do. It is a name we have won in the flames of battle . . . I see flying above us the Red Banner with the five letters which are sacred to us—RSFSR. We, delegates to the Tenth Congress of Soviets, plenipotentiary representatives of the whole Soviet Russian Federation, dip this cherished banner, battle-scarred and covered with glory, strengthened by the sacrifices of the workers and peasants, before the Union of Soviet Republics. We already visualise the raising of the new Red Banner of the Union of Soviet Republics. Comrades, in my mind's eye I see Comrade Lenin holding this banner. And so, comrades, let us go forward, raising this banner higher for all the working and oppressed peoples of the world to see."

For half a century now the victorious Red Banner of the Union of Soviet Socialist Republics has been proudly flying, symbolising the greatness of the communist ideals—the ideals of social justice, peace, friendship, and the fraternal cooperation of nations. This banner has inspired us in labour and in battle, in days of great jubilation and in the hour of grave ordeal. Our present jubilee is, in a manner of speaking, a solemn vow given by the whole Soviet people, a vow of loyalty to our glorious banner, of loyalty to our great Union, a vow of loyalty to the sacred ideals of communism!

## II.

# THE UNBREAKABLE UNITY AND FRATERNAL FRIENDSHIP OF THE PEOPLES OF THE USSR—A GREAT GAIN OF SOCIALISM

Comrades, the joining of all the peoples of the country into a single union—the formation of one multinational socialist state—has opened up unprecedented opportunities for our country's social, economic and cultural progress. It was as if history had itself quickened its march.

Comrades, consider this point. Since the establishment of the Soviet Union the industrial output of the country has increased 320-fold. Some may say, of course, that any comparison with 1922 is not a fair indication, because it was a year of postwar ruin and famine. That is true. So let us compare 1972 with the pre-war year of 1940, the year by which our country had already well surpassed the pre-revolutionary level. In that period alone, the Soviet Union's industrial output increased 14-fold. And now Soviet industry turns out in one month more than it did in the whole of 1940.

The Soviet Union's rapid economic growth has created a reliable basis for a steady rise in the standard of living and in the cultural level of all the peoples of this country. Compared with 1940, the real incomes of the population have increased by more than 300 per cent, while retail sales have increased by over 600 per cent. The number of doctors in the country has increased by 370 per cent, and the number of citizens with a higher, or complete or incomplete secondary education, by 550 per cent.

Behind these figures lie fundamental changes in the economy, in socio-political relations, ideology and culture, which have changed the face of the whole of our society. And an important place among these changes is held by the new, socialist relations that prevail among all the peoples of our country.

Our Party was well aware that if all the consequences of national oppression and inequality were to be overcome there would be need for more than the adoption of even the best and the most equitable laws. There was also need to overcome the economic and cultural backwardness of the once oppressed nations and nationalities. In other words, it was not enough to abolish the legal inequality of nations; it was also necessary to put an end to the actual inequality between them. Fulfilment of this task became one of the Party's main political goals.

Summing up the heroic accomplishments of the past half-century, we have every reason to say that the national question, as it came down to us from the past, has been settled completely, finally and for good. This is an accomplishment which can by rights be ranked on a par with the victories in building the new society in the USSR, such as industrialisation, collectivisation and the cultural revolution.

A great brotherhood of working people, united, irrespective of their national origins, by a community of class interests and aims, has emerged and has been consolidated in this country, the relations between them have no equal in history and we have every right to call these relations the Leninist friendship of peoples. This friendship, comrades, is one of our invaluable gains, one of the most important gains of socialism which is most dear to the heart of every Soviet citizen. We Soviet people will always safeguard this friendship as our most cherished possession!

At present, on this fiftieth anniversary of the Union, the

solution of the national question and the overcoming of the backwardness of the once oppressed nations are regarded by the Soviet people as an ordinary thing, something to be taken for granted. However, we must recall the scale and the complexity of the work that has been done in order to appreciate, not only the wisdom but also the courage and the consistent effort of the Bolshevik Party, which set itself this goal and achieved it.

Let us recall for a moment the state of the outlying national areas of the country by the time of the Revolution. In economic development Central Asia and Kazakhstan were on a level quite usual for colonial countries. Poverty, disease, and ignorance were the lot of the bulk of the population. Suffice it to say that even in the early 1920s from 90 to 96 per cent of the people in the Central Asian Republics and 82 per cent in Kazakhstan could neither read nor write. The social structure there was essentially feudal.

The mark of economic backwardness also lay on many areas of Transcaucasia and even on Byelorussia, which was close to the centre. All these areas, with the exception of a few large cities, still remained in the remote ages in economic terms, and in the social make-up, cultural level and living conditions of the working people.

Indeed, comrades, such was the picture no more than half a century ago, a time witnessed by millions of men and women who are still with us. That is the point at which we had to start, and, furthermore, we were the first to do so, because the proletariat of Russia and its Party had no one's experience to fall back on in tackling these most complicated tasks. The plain fact is that such experience simply was not there.

Those are the conditions in which the Party took, on Lenin's initiative, the line of accelerated economic, cultural, and socio-political development of the outlying national areas.

The Party was aware that this task could be successfully carried out only with great and all-round assistance to the once oppressed nations and nationalities by the more advanced parts of the country, above all, by the Russian people and its working class.

Such assistance, and the readiness to put in a great effort and even, let us plainly say, to make sacrifices so as to overcome the backwardness of the national outskirts and help them to develop at an accelerated pace was bequeathed by Lenin to the proletariat of Russia as a prime internationalist duty. The Russian working class and the Russian people have fulfilled this duty with honour. This was, in effect, a great achievement by a whole class, a whole people, performed in the name of internationalism. This heroic exploit will never be forgotten by the peoples of our country.

The history of this exploit began literally from the earliest days of the Revolution. As early as 1918, Soviet Russia, herself starving and in ruins, allocated tens of millions of rubles for irrigation works in Turkestan. While the Civil War was still being fought, decisions were taken to send food supplies and to extend financial and technical aid to Azerbaijan; sizable funds were remitted to the railwaymen of Kharkov and the miners of the Donets Basin, and important assistance was given to the economy of Byelorussia, Armenia, and Soviet Lithuania and Latvia.

The Tenth Congress of our Party, which concentrated on the tasks of peaceful construction, noted in its resolution: "Now that the landowners and the bourgeoisie have been overthrown . . . , the Party's task is to help the working masses of the non-Russian peoples to catch up with the more advanced Central Russia." One of the directives issued by the Congress in this context was "the planned implantation of industry on the outskirts through a transfer of factories to the sources of raw materials." In accordance with this many factories and plants were transferred, without charge, to the Republics of Transcaucasia, Central Asia and to Kazakhstan, and engineers, technicians, skilled workers, specialists, scientists, teachers and workers in culture were sent to these Republics.

The formation of the USSR marked a new stage in the development of the outlying national areas. Consistent and all-round assistance was rendered to them within the framework of an all-Union economic policy. Suffice it to say that for many years the budget expenditures of a number of the Union Republics were covered mainly by subsidies from the all-Union budget. For instance, in 1924 and 1925 only a little over 10 per cent of the revenues in the budget of the Turkmen Republic was contributed by that republic itself. Even a large republic such as the Ukraine at that time covered under 40 per cent of its budget expenditures with its own resources.

For many years the population in the Republics and regions facing the gravest material hardships was fully or partially exempted from agricultural and civic taxes. At the same time, the purchasing prices of farm produce were set at a level designed to promote the economic development of the once backward regions.

Tremendous assistance was given to the fraternal Union Republics in cultural development, in education and in the training of personnal. Large contingents of young men and women from the national Republics, regions and areas were enrolled at institutions of higher learning in the country's major centres. Dozens of universities and institutes were opened in the Republics. By the will of the Party the socialist cultural revolution rapidly spread to the remotest areas.

The efforts of the Party and the State over a period of many years yielded remarkable fruit. Look at Central Asia and Kazakhstan today! You will find more than first-class cotton fields in Uzbekistan and Turkmenia, the once fallow lands of the Kazakhs under crop, and flowering orchards and new livestock farms in Kirghizia and Tajikistan. Today, these Repub lics are famed for a host of big, modern, beautiful cities, such as Tashkent, Alma-Ata, Dushambe, Frunze and Ashkhabad. There you will find large centres of metallurgy, mining and heavy industry, such as Jezkazgan and Karaganda, Pavlodar and Navoi and first-rate power and water installations, such as the Nurek hydroelectric power station and the Karakum canal. Central Asia and Kazakhstan have become major producers of oil and gas, chemicals and modern machines.

Since the formation of the Union, Kazakhstan's industrial output has increased 600-fold, Tajikistan's over 500-fold. Kirghizia's over 400-fold, Uzbekistan's about 240-fold and Turkmenia's over 130-fold. The gross cotton crop in Uzbekistan has gone up 120-fold and in Turkmenia 90-fold. Kazakhstan now produces almost 30 times more grain than it did in 1922.

The cultural development of Kazakhstan and the Central Asian Republics is equally striking. They have achieved virtually 100 per cent literacy. Almost half the population in each Republic are men and women with a higher or secondary (complete or incomplete) education. In Uzbekistan alone there are now more specialists with a higher or secondary special education than the Soviet Union had working in its economy in the late 1920's. Modern science has been firmly established in these Republics, and in their national academies there are thousands of scientists engaged in valuable research.

In the capitalist world achievements which are much more modest are frequently labelled as "miracles." But we Communists do not consider what has happened in Soviet Central Asia and Soviet Kazakhstan as being in any way supernatural. You might say that it is a natural miracle, because it is natural under Soviet power, under socialism, in conditions of relations of friendship and brotherhood of nations that have been established in this country.

Evidence of this comes not only from Central Asia and Kazakhstan. In Soviet times the Transcaucasian Republics—Georgia, Azerbaijan and Armenia—have also made enormous economic progress. Each of them now has the most modern industries, and they have achieved great successes in their subtropical agriculture. The ancient culture and art of the Transcaucasian peoples have flourished and have been enriched. They have large scientific centres, which are known all over the country.

Byelorussia, which suffered enormous losses in its terrible ordeal during the Great Patriotic War, has flourished in the fraternal family of the Soviet peoples. Fine cities and villages have been rebuilt and major industrial construction projects have been completed in Byelorussia, where the invaders trod the scorched earth during the war. Today, Byelorussia's industries make excellent computers, heavy-duty lorries, modern radio equipment, mineral fertilisers and synthetic fibre. The Republic has a large contingent of scientists and workers in the cultural sphere.

Not long ago Moldavia was also a backward outlying area. If we do not count the war years and the early post-war years spent in rehabilitation, we find that this Republic has been developing in the family of Soviet nations for not more than a quarter-century. But in that short span it has gone a long way! The Republic has become one of the country's granaries, and one of its principal centres of horticulture and wine-making. Its industrial output has increased 31-fold.

In short, on the basis of the Leninist national policy, as a result of the intense efforts of the whole Soviet people we have achieved a state in which the term "backward national outlying area," a common one for old Russia, has disappeared. Comrades, this is a splendid achievement of our Party, an achievement of socialism and of the socialist friendship of nations!

It has benefited the once oppressed and backward nations in this country. It has benefited our great Soviet Motherland, because it has made the Union of Soviet Socialist Republics even more powerful and more firmly united, because it has made the unity of the fraternal Republics truly unbreakable.

The socialist system and the relations of friendship and brotherhood between the nations have also made possible the rapid development of the republics and regions which by the time of the Revolution were already at a relatively high level of economic development.

Among these is the Ukraine which used to be one of the developed industrial and agricultural areas of the country. Ukrainian culture had long and rich traditions. But the Soviet Ukraine has gone such a long way since then!

Take our famous working-class Donets Basin. Let us recall the old coal-mining town of Yuzovka with its huts, dirt and squalor. Compare it with the Yuzovka of today, the large modern city of Donetsk, with its broad avenues and green parks, blocks of modern flats, fine stadiums and Palaces of Culture. Let us recall the life of the Donets Basin miner before the Revolution and the horrible conditions in which he lived and worked. Compare this with the life of the Donets Basin or Krivoy Rog miner today, a man who takes pride in his trade, commanding the respect of the whole country, who is properly paid for his fine labour and enjoys all the benefits of modern culture. Similar comparisons are suggested everywhere: in Zaporozhye, Kharkov and Dnepropetrovsk, in the Kherson and the Transcarpathian areas.

Since the formation of the USSR, industrial output in the Ukraine has increased 176-fold. The present-day Ukraine has a powerful metallurgical industry, a diversified engineering industry, a large-scale ship-building industry and well-developed chemical and food industries and light industry. The Soviet Ukraine also has a large-scale and highly mechanised agriculture. On top of all this there are also splendid scientific centres and magnificent achievements in culture and the arts.

All this is the result of the great effort of the Ukrainian working people and also the result of their fraternal co-operation with the working people of all the other Republics of the Soviet Union. It is no exaggeration to say that the people of the Ukraine have been able to rise to their full stature and to give full scope to their energy and talents only in the community of the Soviet Republics, the union which has enabled them to multiply their own strength!

Another graphic example is offered by the Baltic Republics: Lithuania, Latvia and Estonia. It may be recalled that when they joined the Union they could not be ranked among the backward outlying national areas. But on taking the socialist path they showed the highest rate of development in the Soviet Union. Compared with 1940, industrial output has gone up 31-fold in Latvia, 32-fold in Estonia and 37-fold in Lithuania. Their agriculture made good headway, and their culture flourished after it had shaken off the fetters of provincialism and stagnation in the backwoods of capitalist Europe. This remarkable growth proved possible only when these Republics united with the other Republics of the Union.

I should like to deal specially with the results of the development of the Russian Federation, our biggest Republic, the first among equals, as it is by rights called by all the peoples of our multinational country.

This Republic has had a special historical role to play. On the one hand, as the largest and most developed Republic, it became the mainstay in the development of the other Republics and gave them invaluable fraternal assistance. On the other hand, the Russian Federation is not just Moscow, Leningrad, Gorky and Central Russia's other old industrial towns. It is also a Republic which inherited from the past its own backward national areas. Its 16 Autonomous Republics, 5 autonomous regions and 10 national areas gained their statehood for the first time under Soviet power. On the territory of the Russian Federation there are dozens of peoples, including many which were threatened with extinction under tsarism.

Moreover, together with the large industrial and cultural centres, many fundamentally Russian areas inherited from tsarist Russia old, backward out-of-the-way places, the countless provincial townlets and stagnant hamlets described with bitterness and pain by the Russian classical writers.

That is why efforts in various directions were required to promote the development of the Russian Federation. There was the need for rapid progress in the most advanced centres and regions which have played the role of the main base, and continue to do so, ensuring the advance of the whole of Soviet society. At the same time it was necessary to overcome backwardness over a large area of the Republic, to solve the national question, or to be more precise, a multiplicity of national questions inherited from the past in the Federation itself. Finally, there were the vast territories in Siberia, the Far East and the North to be opened up.

The working people of the RSFSR fulfilled these great tasks

with honour. Hundreds of new modern cities and industrial centres have arisen across the Republic on either side of the Urals. The Republic's old major cities, beginning with Moscow, our capital, and Leningrad, the cradle of the Revolution, have been rejuvenated. Rich deposits of oil, gas, coal, metallic ores, gold and diamonds have been discovered and placed at the service of society.

The Federation's industry has made giant strides: in the 50 years its output has increased by more than 300-fold, going up by more than 11 times during the post-war years alone. Just imagine what this means, considering the vast scale of the Republic's economy. The output of staple farm produce has been doubled and trebled. Soviet Russia's achievements in science, culture and education are also well known.

Comrades, our half-century of experience is graphic confirmation of Lenin's ideas about the advantages offered by a large-scale, centralised national economy as compared with a fragmented economy. The pooling of the economic potentials and resources of all the Republics accelerates the development of each, the smallest and the largest alike. Management and planning of the economy on a Union scale have made it possible to effect a rational location of the productive forces; they afford scope for economic manoeuvre, and have helped to enhance co-operation and specialisation, which yield an overall benefit well in excess of a mere arithmetical addition of the individual efforts of each Republic, region and district.

This path has been tested, it is reliable, and we shall advance along it towards new achievements, towards fresh gains in communist construction.

On the basis of the deep-going and all-round socio-political changes over the past half-century our society has risen to a qualitatively new level, thereby realising the prediction of our great leader, Lenin, who held that socialism "creates new and superior forms of human society." Indeed, as the 24th Congress of the CPSU noted, *a new historical entity of men—the Soviet people*—has been established and has become a reality in this country.

This entity is based on the deeply-rooted objective material and spiritual changes in the country's life, on the emergence and development in our country of socialist nations which have established a new type of relations among themselves.

The economy of the Soviet Union is not the sum total of the economies of the individual republics and regions. It has long since become one economic organism, formed on the basis of the common economic aims and interests of all our nations and nationalities.

The state of economic affairs in, say, Uzbekistan depends not only on the cotton crop in the Republic itself, but also on the work of the machine-builders of the Urals and Leningrad, the miners of the Kuznetsk Basin, the grain-growing state farms of Kazakhstan and the makers of electronic computers in Byelorussia. Similarly, the prosperity of the Ukraine depends not only on the success of the work done there, but also on the results achieved in the oil industry of Tataria and Bashkiria, the timber industry in the Komi Autonomous Republic, the engineering industry in Moscow, Gorky and Kuibyshev. There are hundreds and thousands of similar examples. The scale of our work tends to overstep the boundaries not only of economic regions but also of the Union Republics.

In the past fifty years radical changes have also taken place in the sphere of social relations. In the Soviet Union, the exploitation of man by man has long since been eliminated. The entire Soviet people now consists of socialist classes and social groups. It is welded together by common purpose and outlook. Communism is its goal, and Marxism-Leninism the basis of its world outlook.

There have been marked changes in the working class, the chief productive force of society and the most progressive class of the present epoch, the collective-farm peasantry, which has shed the private-property mentality, and the Soviet intelligentsia, whose whole creative effort is dedicated to the cause of communist construction.

All the Republics, Union and Autonomous, and all the national regions and areas now have large contingents of the working class. It is the working class, by nature the most internationalist class of all, that plays the decisive role in the process of bringing closer together all the nations and nationalities in our country. It is the workers of all nationalities, belonging to close-knit production collectives, that are putting up industrial projects regardless of where they may be located, building the railways, and digging the canals, laying the oil pipelines and erecting the electric-power transmission lines linking the various parts of the country, the Union and the Autonomous Republics, and the territories and regions into one economic whole.

In each of the Soviet Republics, in each region and in each major city you will find men and women of many nationalities living as neighbours and working together. Throughout the country there is a growing number of mixed marriages, which now run into millions.

As the economic and social development of each national Republic is intensified, the internationalisation of every aspect of our life in these Republics becomes more pronounced. Take Soviet Kazakhstan, which has been growing so rapidly. Besides the Kazakhs, millions of Russians, hundreds of thousands of Ukrainians, Uzbeks, Byelorussians and people of other nationalities live there. Kazakh culture is developing and becoming richer as it absorbs the best elements of Russian, Ukrainian, and other national cultures. Is this good or bad? We Communists confidently say: it is good, it is very good, indeed!

In the half-century of the USSR, a Soviet socialist culture has emerged and flourished in this country, a culture that is identical in spirit and basic content, embodying the most valuable features and traditions of the culture and life of each Soviet nation. At the same time, not a single Soviet national culture draws only on its own resources: it also assimilates the spiritual riches of the other fraternal nations and, in turn, contributes to these cultures and enriches them.

Common, internationalist features are becoming ever more pronounced in the varied national forms of Soviet socialist culture. In a progressive process, the national culture is increasingly enriched by the achievements of the other fraternal nations. This process is in the spirit of socialism and in the interest of all the nations of our country, laying the groundwork for a new, communist culture that is devoid of national barriers and equally serves all men of labour.

We already have good reason to say that Soviet culture is socialist in content and in its main trend of development, is varied in national form and internationalist in spirit and character. It is thus an organic fusion of the spiritual riches being created by all the Soviet nations.

Comrades, these are no abstract formulas: this is life itself. In Turkmenia or Moldavia, for instance, tens and hundreds of thousands read and appreciate Pushkin, Shevchenko, Gorky, Mayakovsky, Sholokhov, Tvardovsky, Fedin and Stelmakh as they do their own national writers, while the Russian or the Ukrainian has adopted, as part of his own cultural heritage, the ancient but never-aging epos of Shota Rustaveli, the fine works of Vilis Lacis, Abai Kunanbayev, and Chinghiz Aitmatov and the splendid poetry of Yanka Kupala, Samed Vurgun, Rasul Gamzatov, Eduardas Meželaitis, Mustai Karim, and many, many others.

The rapid growth of bonds and co-operation between the Soviet nations and nationalities serves to enhance the importance of the Russian language, which has now become the linguistic medium of mutual communication for all of them. And of course, comrades, we are all glad to see that Russian has become one of the universally accepted world languages.

Thus, both materially and culturally there is a breakdown of national barriers—a process which Lenin time and again described as important—providing the prerequisites for a further drawing together of the Soviet nations. The powerful source of their unity lies in the common history of the Soviet people as a whole and all its constituent nations and national groups, and the common traditions, attitudes and experience stemming from the half-century of their joint struggle and joint labour.

The heroic exploits in defence of the socialist Motherland were the most convincing expression of the Soviet people's unity. The union and friendship of all its nations and nationalities withstood the grim trials of the Great Patriotic War, during which the sons and daughters of the same Soviet Motherland not only succeeded in safeguarding with honour their socialist gains, but also saved world civilisation from the barbarity of fascism, thereby lending powerful support to the peoples' liberation struggle. The glory of this country's heroes, its valiant defenders, will not dim through the ages.

Today, our Armed Forces reliably guard the socialist Motherland, protecting its people's peaceful labour in building communism. The Soviet people deeply respect and love their army, because they know that they need a well-equipped army as long as forces of aggression still exist in the world. The Soviet Army is also a special kind of army in that it is a school of internationalism, a school that fosters feelings of brotherhood, solidarity, and mutual respect among all Soviet nations and nationalities. Our Armed Forces are one friendly family, a real embodiment of socialist internationalism.

Apart from their glorious military record, Soviet people of every nationality are also brought together by the legendary feats of the shock workers in the early five-year-plan periods, the heroic labour of postwar rehabilitation, the exploits of the men and women who developed the virgin lands, the unprecedented scale of the great construction projects of our day, and the opening up of the northern and eastern areas. Joint labour and struggle have forged the Soviet people's common traditions, which are a source of pride and are cherished by every Soviet citizen.

The emergence in our country of a new historical entity of men, the Soviet people, is our great accomplishment, comrades. We are justified in regarding it as the epitome of the economic and socio-political changes that have taken place in this country in the past fifty years.

Lenin's Party, its collective reason and unbending will, its organising and guiding role, was the force that paved the way for the formation of the great Union of Soviet Socialist Republics, a force that has guided its development over the half-century, and that is now confidently leading it forward.

The CPSU is a Party of Leninist internationalists both in ideology and policy, and in structure and composition.

The Bolshevik Party was the first political party based on the principle of uniting proletarian organisations in which workers of different nationalities formed a single fighting force. V. I. Lenin wrote back in 1905: "To dispel any idea of its being national in character, the Party called itself 'Rossiiskaya' and not 'Russkaya.'"/The adjective Russkaya (Russian) pertains to nationality, Rossiiskaya (Russian) pertains to Russia as a country—Ed./ Upon the formation of the Soviet Union, the Party emphasised this special feature by changing its name first to "All-Union Communist Party (Bolsheviks)" and then to "Communist Party of the Soviet Union."

The Party unites the foremost representatives of all the country's nations and nationalities. It is the most vivid embodiment of the Soviet working people's friendship and militant comradeship, the inviolable unity of the entire Soviet people. All Communists in this country, regardless of nationality, are members of the single Leninist Party. All of them enjoy equal rights, have equal duties, and bear equal responsibility for the country's destiny.

It is to the Party's credit that millions upon millions of Soviet men of every nation and nationality have adopted internationalism—once the ideal of a handful of Communists—as their profound conviction and principle of behaviour. This was a true revolution in social thinking, and one which is hard to overestimate. The Party's success is largely due to its implacable attitude to any departures from the Leninist national policy within its ranks, its resolute struggle against all manner of deviations, its firm stand with regard to the great Marxist-Leninist theory and its creative development.

Lenin is known to have repeatedly emphasised the complexity of tackling national problems, the need to show tact and tolerance with respect to national feelings, those of the smaller nations in particular, and the need gradually to foster in the latter the spirit of internationalism. But Lenin always demanded that the *Communists* of any nationality should take a clear and principled stand on the national question, and never allowed any indulgence in this matter. He always waged a relentless struggle against any manifestations of nationalism or great-power chauvinism among Communists.

Is it in place, some may ask, to talk of such problems now that our multinational socialist state has been in existence for 50 years and has been developing successfully, now that the Soviet people have started to build communist society? Yes, comrades, it is in place.

As I have already mentioned, we have successfully dealt with those aspects of the national problem that we inherited from the pre-revolutionary past. But in a mature socialist society, national relations continue to be a constantly developing reality, which keeps posing new tasks and problems. The Party never loses sight of these questions, tackling them in due time in the interests of the country as a whole and of every Republic in particular, in the interests of communist construction.

It should be remembered that nationalistic prejudices, exaggerated or distorted national feelings, are extremely tenacious and deeply embedded in the psychology of politically immature people. These prejudices survive even when the objective premises for any antagonisms in relations between nations have long since ceased to exist. It should also be borne in mind that nationalistic tendencies are often intertwined with parochial attitudes, which are akin to nationalism.

Neither can we afford to overlook the fact that nationalistic survivals are being encouraged in every way from outside the country—by politicians and propagandists of the bourgeois world. Our class adversaries zestfully seize on all cases of this kind, inflaming and encouraging them in the hope of undermining—if only a little—the unity of the peoples of our country.

Lastly, comrades, there are also objective problems in our

federal state, such as finding the most correct way of developing the individual nations and nationalities and the most correct balance between the interests of each nation and nationality and the common interests of the Soviet people as a whole. In dealing with these problems, our Party closely follows Lenin's injunction that the maximum concern be shown for the development and interests of each nation.

The further drawing together of the nations and nationalities of our country is an objective process. The Party is against hastening the process: there is no need for that, since it is determined by the entire course of our Soviet life. At the same time, the Party considers it impermissible to attempt in any way to hold it up, to impede it on some pretext, or to give undue emphasis to national distinctiveness, because this would go against the general line of development of our society, the internationalist ideals and the ideology of Communists, the interests of communist construction.

Lenin could not have been more explicit on this score: "The proletariat cannot support any consecration of nationalism; on the contrary, it supports everything that helps to obliterate national distinctions and remove national barriers; it supports everything that makes the ties between nationalities closer and closer."

As the Party resolves the problems of the country's further development along the way mapped out by Lenin, it attaches great importance to the continuous, systematic and deep-going education of all Soviet citizens in the spirit of internationalism and Soviet patriotism. For us these two concepts comprise an indivisible whole. Needless to say that they are fostered in the people by the Soviet way of life, by all our reality. But it also requires the conscious efforts of the Party, of everyone working on the politico-ideological front. Our effort in this regard is an extremely important part of the general effort of building communism.

Comrades, the accomplishments of the past 50 years are a source of pride for all Soviet people, giving us firm confidence in the future of our great Motherland.

The path traversed in this half-century instills in us faith in the strength of our Party, our state, our fine people. If the obstacles that faced us in the past failed to stem our victorious march to socialism, then no one and nothing can block our path now that the Soviet Union has scaled such heights. All the goals set by the Party of Lenin are certain to be attained.

The mighty winds of the times, the winds of history, are filling the sails of the ship of socialism. And indomitably our ship is sailing farther and farther ahead to the radiant horizons of communism.

# III.

## THE SOVIET UNION IS A DEPENDABLE BULWARK IN THE PEOPLES' STRUGGLE FOR PEACE, NATIONAL INDEPENDENCE AND SOCIALISM

Comrades, during the half-century of the Soviet Union's existence the world has witnessed socio-political changes of unprecedented scale and depth.

The socialist revolution triumphed in a number of countries in Europe, Asia and America giving rise to a world socialist system. In the capitalist world, the international working-class movement became a mighty, well-organised and politically active force. And its militant vanguard—Communist and Workers' Parties—came into being and grew in most countries of the world. Imperialism's system of colonial oppression collapsed for good.

In short, the world has changed in this half-century. And it is an indisputable fact, comrades, that the Soviet Union—the very fact of its existence, the example of our socialist society, the dynamic foreign policy of our state—has played no small part in all these historic changes.

Life has completely borne out the conclusion drawn by our great leader, Lenin, that the Union of Soviet Socialist Republics and its consolidation are necessary "for the world Communist proletariat in its struggle against the world bourgeoisie and its defence against bourgeois intrigues."

Today, the "world Communist proletariat," the fraternal socialist countries, the Communist Parties, the progressive revolutionary-democratic organisations, the trade unions and broadest sections of working people in all continents have joined us in celebrating the 50th anniversary of the Soviet Union.

We are deeply grateful to our comrades and allies in the fraternal socialist countries, to people who share our beliefs and friends in other countries, for their kind sentiments and solidarity. Throughout our country's history we have had occasion time and again to appreciate how important for us is our alliance with the international working class and with the communist movement, how important is the support by upright, progressive people across the world for our peace-loving policy. We highly value this support.

On this momentous occasion we again assure our comrades-in-arms, our class brothers, our friends all over the world that the Soviet Union shall always be faithful to the great cause of the international unity of the fighters for the freedom of the peoples, for socialism, for lasting world peace.

As we see it, the purpose of our foreign policy is to strengthen peace, which we need for building communism, which is required by all socialist countries, by the peoples of all lands. This is why we shall continue to counteract the policy of aggression and help to eliminate throughout the world the conditions that breed aggressive wars.

As we see it, it is the purpose and mission of our foreign policy to help all the peoples to exercise their inalienable rights and, above all, their right to independent and sovereign development, so that they may benefit from the fruits of modern civilisation.

As we see it, the purpose and mission of our policy on the international scene is to side unfailingly with those who are fighting imperialism and all forms of exploitation and oppression, for freedom and human dignity, for democracy and socialism.

In short, we cherish the freedom, peace and well-being of our people, and we want all the peoples of the world to enjoy freedom, peace and well-being.

Comrades, our foreign policy has always been and will continue to be a class policy, a socialist one in content and aim. And it is precisely its socialist character that makes it a peace policy. "We know, we know only too well, the incredible misfortunes that war brings to the workers and peasants," Lenin stressed. Lenin's conclusion was crystal clear: to safeguard peace by all means; having started peaceful construction, to make every effort to continue it without interruption. The Soviet state has always followed this course charted by Lenin. From the first foreign-policy act of Soviet power—the Decree on Peace—to the Peace Programme of the 24th Congress of the CPSU, our Party and state have steadily adhered to the main guidelines of struggle for peace and for the freedom and security of the peoples.

For nearly a quarter of a century—nearly half the life of the federal Soviet state—we have no longer been alone and have forged ahead together with the fraternal countries. We have repeatedly declared that we consider it our prime international task to consolidate and develop the world socialist system.

In the early and most difficult years of the People's Democracies, the Soviet Union played the decisive part in defending them against imperialist interference, and on many occasions gave them the necessary political and economic support. Later, too, joint defence against imperialism's hostile sallies, against its attempts to undermine the socialist system in one country or another, continued, and continues, to be one of the important prerequisites for the successful development of the world socialist system.

As a result of collective efforts and hard-fought battles against the class enemy we forged a lasting alliance of socialist states and a dependable system of all-round fraternal co-operation, which has become, as it were, the natural way of life for each of our countries. We have learned to carry on our day-to-day tasks successfully, to patiently arrive at suitable solutions of issues that cannot be resolved in capitalist conditions. And in doing this, we have learned to harmonise the interests of each with the interests of all and to co-operate, sweeping aside everything that may hinder or complicate the joint progress.

When the question of uniting the Soviet Republics in a single Union of Soviet Socialist Republics arose 50 years ago, Lenin pointed out that the Union was necessary in order to withstand the military onslaught of imperialism, to defend the gains of the Revolution, and to accomplish the peaceful creative tasks of socialist construction more successfully by common effort.

In principle, the same applies to the fraternal community of sovereign socialist states that belong to the Warsaw Treaty Organisation and the Council for Mutual Economic Assistance. This community was formed primarily to counter the imperialist threat, the aggressive imperialist military blocs, and to safeguard in common the cause of socialism and peace. And we have every reason to declare that never have socialism's positions been as firm as they are today, and that the cause of peace is gaining one victory after another.

But even in the present conditions, far from diminishing, the need for unity and the closest co-operation among socialist countries has become even greater. Today we require unity, co-operation and joint action chiefly in order to accomplish more quickly and effectively the tasks of developing socialist society and building communism. Moreover, we require unity, cohesion and co-operation in order to attain the best results in safeguarding and consolidating the peace, so vital for all the peoples, to further the international détente, and to effectively repulse all aggressive sallies of the imperialists, all attempts to impinge on the interests of socialism.

This is why the Soviet Union has always been and always

will be an active champion of unity and co-operation among all the socialist countries.

Comrades, today one feels impelled to make special mention of our relations with that fraternal socialist state which has become for the whole world the symbol of heroic struggle against aggression. I am referring to the Democratic Republic of Vietnam.

In Washington the Vietnam war is described as the longest in American history. That is true. It should be added, however, that it is also the dirtiest of all wars in American history.

Now, the world has witnessed new American imperialist crimes in Vietnam. Apart from the fact that by resorting to various unsavoury manoeuvres, the United States is artificially delaying the conclusion of an agreement on terminating the war, some days ago it again began to bomb towns and mine ports in the Democratic Republic of Vietnam.

Grave responsibility devolves on the US government for these barbarian acts and for the blood of the Vietnamese people that it continues to shed. Like all the peace-loving states, like all the peoples of the world, the Soviet Union firmly and indignantly condemns these acts of aggression.

It is clear to everyone by now that the US military venture in Vietnam has failed. And no new outrages can break the will of the heroic people of Vietnam or make their friends waver in their determination to give them every possible support and aid in their just liberation struggle.

No matter what senseless brutalities the modern colonialists may commit, imperialism no longer possesses its former ability to dispose of the destiny of the peoples unimpeded. The socialist cause, the national liberation movement are invincible. In our time, the international solidarity of the socialist states, of all revolutionaries, of all fighters for peace and progress, has become a tremendous force.

We could say a great deal about our military, economic and other aid to fighting Vietnam. But our Vietnamese friends, the leaders of the Democratic Republic of Vietnam and the Provisional Revolutionary Government of the Republic of South Vietnam, do so much more convincingly.

One other point needs to be stressed. We have always regarded it as a cardinal objective of the Soviet Union's foreign policy to seek to eliminate the seat of war in Indochina. This is why we give our Vietnamese friends active assistance in their efforts for a just peace settlement.

In short, we are manifesting our internationalist solidarity with the people of Vietnam by concrete deeds all along the line. And we shall spare no effort to preserve and strengthen Soviet-Vietnamese friendship.

Now, comrades, a few words about our present relations with China or, rather, about China's attitude towards most of the socialist states.

It is more than ten years since the leaders of the People's Republic of China have taken the line of struggling against the USSR and, in effect, the entire socialist community, which they continue to regard as the main obstacle to their great-power designs.

Speaking bluntly, what does Peking's foreign policy amount to today? It amounts to absurd claims to Soviet territory, to malicious slander of the Soviet social and political system, of our peace-loving foreign policy. It is outright sabotage of the efforts to limit the arms race, of the efforts to bring about disarmament and a relaxation of international tension. It amounts to constant attempts to split the socialist camp and the communist movement, to foment discord among the fighters for national liberation, to range the developing countries against the Soviet Union and the other socialist states. Lastly, it amounts to unprincipled alignments on anti-Soviet grounds with any, even the most reactionary forces—the most rabid haters of the Soviet Union from among the English Tories or the revenge-seeking elements in the FRG, the Portuguese colonialists or the racists of South Africa.

In substance, the purpose of doing the greatest possible harm to the USSR, of impairing the interests of the socialist community, is now the sole criterion determining the Chinese leaders' approach to any major international problem.

What can one say about this policy?

We hold that it is unnatural for relations between socialist countries, that it runs counter to the interests not only of the Soviet, but also of the Chinese people, it runs counter to the interests of world socialism, of the liberation and anti-imperialist struggle, of peace and international security.

It is therefore understandable why we categorically reject this policy.

The Chinese leaders claim to be disturbed about some threat emanating from the Soviet Union. If these statements are not hypocritical, it is impossible to understand why China has not replied to our proposal, repeatedly made since 1969, to assume clear, firm and permanent commitments ruling out an attack by one country on the other. If Peking is really concerned about China's security, why has not the PRC leadership agreed to conclude a special treaty renouncing the use of force, the draft of which was submitted to the Chinese side on January 15, 1971? The draft of this treaty states unequivocally that the sides—and I quote—"shall not use against each other armed forces employing any type of arms, including: a) conventional, b) missile, or c) nuclear." No, the Chinese leaders' complaints about a mythical "Soviet threat" quite obviously do not stand up to scrutiny.

Our policy toward China is well known. It is outlined clearly in the decisions of the 24th Party Congress. We are pursuing this policy consistently, and shall continue to do so, because it is based on a sober analysis of the present and future realities, and we are convinced that it is correct.

The Soviet Union has neither territorial nor economic claims on China. Soviet people remember that the relations between the USSR and China have by far not always been what they are now. It is common knowledge that our country rendered the Chinese Communists substantial aid in their struggle against the Japanese aggressors and the Chinese bourgeoisie. The part played in the victory of the people's democratic revolution in China by the Soviet Army's defeating the Japanese forces occupying China, is also common knowledge. In China they probably remember that the first international treaty concluded by the newly-established People's Republic of China was the Treaty of Friendship, Alliance and Mutual Assistance with the Soviet Union. They probably still remember also the tremendous aid rendered by the Soviet Union to People's China in building her heavy industry, strengthening her defence might, and training national personnel.

Those were good times in Soviet-Chinese relations, relations that were natural for socialist states. And we trust that the objective interests of the peoples of our two countries and the laws of history will ultimately prevail over the subjective political distortions and that Soviet-Chinese friendship will be restored.

We want to see China a flourishing socialist power, and to work shoulder to shoulder with her for peace, against imperialism. But when this will come about depends on China herself. Nothing, of course, will make us depart from our principled Marxist-Leninist line, from our firm defence of the state interests of the Soviet people and the inviolability of Soviet territory, from our determined struggle against the divisive activities of the PRC leadership in the socialist world and the liberation movement.

Comrades, the whole world knows that acting on Lenin's behests, our Party and people actively support the national liberation struggle of the peoples and the progressive policy of countries liberated from colonial oppression. In saying this we want to stress that in present conditions, as we see it, a policy is progressive if it firmly repulses neocolonialism and promotes the sovereignty and independence of the young states, and their economic liberation from imperialism, and if it is for peace, for social progress and closer solidarity with the other progressive forces of our time, and particularly with the socialist countries.

The Soviet Union is promoting friendly ties and all-round co-operation with the states that share this view.

Friendship between the Soviet Union and India, one of the biggest peace-loving countries on our planet, is exerting a strong, positive influence on the international situation as a whole. By now, the Soviet Union and India have had considerable experience in fruitful co-operation. Now that our relations are based on the Treaty of Peace, Friendship and Co-operation we feel that they will become closer still. This is borne out by the consolidation of the progressive, anti-imperialist forces in India. It is also borne out by the policy of the Indian Government headed by Indira Gandhi.

We are pleased to state that we have good relations with many peace-loving countries in Asia and Africa, and, first and foremost, with our immediate neighbours—Afghanistan, Iran and Turkey. We feel there are good prospects for the promotion of good relations with Bangladesh and Pakistan.

We have broad, many-sided relations with a number of Arab countries. The entire course of events has shown that friendship with the Soviet Union ensures the progressive Arab states the necessary support and aid in their most difficult hour. This is well known in Egypt, Syria, Iraq and the Yemen. We have treaties of friendship with Egypt and Iraq, and shall develop our relations with these countries on the basis of these documents. We are firmly resolved to strengthen friendly ties with Syria, Algeria and other Arab countries, too.

The present international situation is such that all who desire to consolidate world peace should multiply their efforts for extinguishing the hotbed of war in the Middle East and overcoming the consequences of the Israeli aggression against the Arab states. Many countries have come out in favour of resolving the Middle East problems on the basis of the relevant UN Security Council resolutions, but regrettably words are not enough. If they were buttressed by concrete political actions, Israel would be compelled to agree to a peaceful settlement, to recognise the legitimate rights of the Arab peoples. As for the Soviet Union, our readiness to contribute to this is well known.

Our co-operation with many Latin American countries has

been making considerable headway of late. Beyond question, this is a result of the consolidation of their independence and of far-reaching anti-imperialist and democratic changes in those countries. Convincing evidence of these changes is provided by the marked strengthening in Latin America of the political positions of heroic revolutionary Cuba, whose leader, our dear friend and comrade, Fidel Castro, we are happy to welcome in this hall today.

Recently, Salvador Allende, President of the Republic of Chile, paid a friendly visit to our country. We regard the results of our talks with the head of that state, which has firmly taken the path of anti-imperialist policy and social progress, as a new important step in the development of our relations. We profoundly sympathise with the freedom struggle of the people of Chile, as we do with the struggle of the peoples of other Latin American countries. We are convinced that this struggle will be successful!

Comrades, it is common knowledge that in many developing countries an acute struggle is under way between the new, progressive forces and internal reaction, which is receiving outside imperialist support. And one of the issues in this struggle is the development of relations with world socialism. Both past experience and current developments show that socio-political conflict in such countries may lead to all kinds of twists and turns. We are well aware of this.

However, patriots in former colonies and semi-colonies have passed a hard political school of national liberation revolutions. And one of the lessons they have learnt is that friendship with the Soviet Union and other socialist countries helps to ensure the success of the struggle against imperialism and to consolidate the genuine independence of the liberated countries.

Comrades, the Peace Programme of the 24th CPSU Congress has proclaimed the Soviet Union's readiness to expand mutually beneficial co-operation in every sphere with countries also seeking such co-operation. As regards Europe, this point is stated still more explicitly: to bring about a radical turn towards détente and peace on that continent.

This completely accords with the common platform of the world communist movement. It is clearly stated in the Document of the 1969 International Meeting of Communist Parties that struggle for world peace is the main aspect of the joint action of Communists.

Only a little over eighteen months have passed since the 24th Congress. But we can confidently say that our Party and the Soviet state have gone a long way in implementing the most important propositions of the Peace Programme.

Together with our friends and allies we have made great efforts to settle problems inherited from the Second World War, and to create a healthier political climate in the world. Our relations with many bourgeois countries, including most countries of capitalist Europe, have shifted towards détente and mutually beneficial co-operation.

Elements of realism in the policy of many capitalist countries are becoming ever more pronounced as the might and influence of the USSR and the fraternal socialist countries increase, as our peace-loving policy becomes more active, and as other important progressive processes successfully unfold in the modern world. First and foremost, this applies to France, whose leaders—General de Gaulle and, later, President Pompidou—some years ago took a definite course of mutually advantageous co-operation with the Soviet Union and other socialist states. This applies to the Federal Republic of Germany, the realistic foreign policy of whose government, headed by Chancellor Brandt, has had a considerable influence on the situation in Europe. This also applies to the United States of America in so far as it shows a willingness to depart from many of the cold-war dogmas that had for so long determined the orientation of all American foreign policy.

In other words, our consistent policy of peace and the entire course of events are gradually making the capitalist world recognise the necessity of dealing with the socialist states on the basis of peaceful coexistence.

The treaties between the USSR and the FRG, and between Poland and the FRG, which formalised the inviolability of the existing European frontiers, the set of agreements on West Berlin, and the treaty on the principles governing relations between the GDR and the FRG, which is being signed today in the GDR capital, the final break-through of the diplomatic blockade of the GDR—all these are important steps in Europe's progress towards peace and security. And all this is not any one country's gain alone, but a big victory for reason and realism in international relations.

To be sure, there remain international problems in Europe which still await a solution. Take problems like the invalidation of the Munich *diktat,* and the admission of the GDR and the FRG to the United Nations. Their solution would help successfully to complete the process of clearing international relations in Europe of all the elements that have burdened them throughout the postwar period.

Our people know that the two world wars burst into their homes from the West, from Europe. We remember 1941. Every Soviet citizen cherishes the memory of the 20 million compatriots who laid down their lives in the Great Patriotic War. We remember all this well as we complete the history-making work of finalising the immutability of the postwar European settlement. And we may rightly say today that none of the results of the anti-fascist liberation struggle of the peoples has been forfeited; the fruits of the great victory have been preserved and consolidated!

The Soviet Union will persevere in its policy of securing a durable peace in Europe, the policy which we have pursued throughout the postwar period and which is now yielding results that gladden the Soviet people and all who cherish peace. We value our good relations with France and will develop them in accordance with the Principles of Co-operation adopted by the two countries last year. We shall continue our efforts to improve and extend our ties with the FRG in various fields. We are prepared to develop all that is positive that has become or is becoming part of the practice of our relations with countries like Finland, our good neighbour, Italy, the Scandinavian nations and a number of other countries. We are also prepared to improve relations with those European countries, with which they are as yet unsmooth—provided, of course, they show by deed a willingness to do the same.

The all-European conference on security and co-operation, for which the socialist countries have worked for many years, should open a new chapter in European history. It appears that the conference will begin not later than the middle of 1973.

The peoples attach great hopes to the convocation of the all-European conference. They expect it to deal with the basic problems of strengthening European peace, to put an end to the suspicion and fear bred by the cold war, and give the Europeans confidence in the morrow. It seems that its success could introduce useful and sound elements into relations between the European countries and the non-European participants in the conference—the United States and Canada.

We shall strive to achieve meaningful results at the conference, which would be of benefit to all its participants.

Everybody knows the political principles which, in the opinion of the USSR and its allies, should constitute the basis for ensuring the security of the European nations. They are: inviolability of state frontiers, non-interference in the internal affairs of other countries, independence, equality, and renunciation of the threat or use of force.

The time has come, we believe, to put on the agenda the elaboration of a European programme of economic and cultural co-operation. This leads to the following question: is it possible to find a basis for some forms of businesslike relations between Europe's two inter-state trade and economic organisations—the Council for Mutual Economic Assistance and the Common Market? It could probably be found, if the Common Market countries refrain from all attempts at discrimination of the other side, and if they help to develop natural bilateral ties and all-European co-operation.

One often hears that the West attaches importance to co-operation in the cultural domain and, especially, to exchange of ideas, extension of information, and to contacts between nations. Permit us to declare here in all earnest: we, too, are in favour of this if, of course, such co-operation is conducted with due respect for the sovereignty, the laws and the customs of each country, and if it promotes mutual spiritual enrichment of the peoples, greater trust between them, and the ideas of peace and good-neighbourliness. We are for broader tourist exchanges. We are for broad public contacts, for meetings between youths, people of related professions, for travel on a collective or individual basis. In short, the possibilities here are quite broad if the matter is dealt with in a spirit of mutual respect and non-interference in each other's affairs, and not in a cold-war spirit.

As is known, negotiations are also to be held on reducing armed forces and armaments in Europe, and, first and foremost, in the area of Central Europe. The Soviet Union favours serious preparations for, and effective conduct of, these negotiations.

The consolidation of European peace is an issue of great importance for the future of all mankind. We are doing our utmost, with all energy and determination, to make it impossible for Europe, which has long been a dangerous volcano, to give rise to another war. We are well aware that reaction, militarism, revanchists of all shades, have not abandoned attempts to reverse the course of events in Europe. But their efforts will fail. The balance of forces on the continent is in favour of peace and peaceful cooperation. And we believe that wars can be eliminated from the life of the European peoples.

Speaking of the Soviet Union's relations with the United States, it will be recalled that the Resolution of the 24th CPSU Congress formulated our objectives as follows:

"The Congress instructs the CC CPSU consistently to continue carrying forward into practice the principle of peaceful coexistence, to extend mutually advantageous relations with the capitalist countries. The Soviet Union is prepared to develop relations also with the United States of America, holding that this conforms with the interests both of the Soviet and the American peoples and those of world peace. At the same time, the Soviet Union will always firmly oppose the aggressive actions of the United States and the policy of force."

As you see, the objectives are quite clear. They are in keeping with the class line of the socialist state's peace-loving policy. The Central Committee of our Party, the Soviet Government, follow this line consistently.

The negotiations we had with President Nixon in Moscow this spring were a big step forward in the development of Soviet-American relations.

What is especially important is that the two sides have jointly defined the principles that are to govern the relations between the USSR and the USA, and that they did so out of a conviction that no foundation other than peaceful coexistence is possible for the relations between the two countries in the nuclear age. This, precisely, is the principal meaning of the pertinent Soviet-American document signed last May.

The readiness expressed by the two sides to co-operate in different fields was accompanied by practical measures. Here I have in mind a whole series of agreements on various matters signed during the summit meeting and during subsequent Soviet-American contacts.

The Soviet-American agreements concerning anti-missile and offensive strategic weapons are, in effect, in physical terms putting a limit, for the first time in history, on these modern and most powerful types of weapons. But we do not intend to stop there. The understanding reached in Moscow should be consolidated and developed. One of the aims of the negotiations on this subject now under way is to find ways of turning the provisional agreement into a permanent one. And it would probably be a good thing if we gave thought to how we could go over from limiting armaments to their gradual reduction, and also to the establishment of some kind of limits to their qualitative development.

We have concluded a series of economic agreements with the United States. Their implementation could create the basis for large-scale and long-term co-operation in this field. At the same time, this could promote a healthier political climate in Soviet-American relations and facilitate further progress towards lasting peace, the main aim of Soviet foreign policy.

If the two countries—the USSR and the USA—will really follow the course charted jointly during the Moscow negotiations, then, we believe, it might be possible to take new substantial steps in developing Soviet-American relations for the benefit of the peoples of the two countries and for universal peace during further contacts. However—and this should be emphatically stressed—much will depend on the course of events in the immediate future, and, in particular, on the turn in the question of ending the war in Vietnam.

Comrades, in conformance with the fundamental principles of our policy of peace, good-neighbourliness and international friendship, the Soviet Union has advanced the idea of a system of collective security in Asia. It is being alleged in some capitals that our proposal is designed to "contain" or "encircle" China. Such allegations are totally groundless. To our way of thinking, the People's Republic of China would become an equal partner in such a system.

Important Soviet-Japanese negotiations are to take place next year. Their purpose is to settle matters pending since the Second World War and to provide a formal treaty basis for relations between our countries. We are striving for a mutually acceptable understanding on all issues under discussion in their entirety. However, it is clear that no positive results in the negotiations can be expected, unless the Japanese side also displays the same willingness. The Soviet Union, for its part, is in favour of truly good-neighbourly relations with Japan.

The Soviet Union has been working for disarmament since the first years of its existence. In the past ten years, a series of important treaties has been concluded with the most active participation of our country on such matters as the banning of nuclear weapons tests, nuclear non-proliferation, the banning of bacteriological weapons and so on. It stands to reason that all these are merely the opening pages of the chronicle of disarmament. We call on all governments, on all the peoples of the world, to fill the succeeding pages of this chronicle jointly, including the last one—general and complete disarmament.

The adoption by the UN General Assembly—also on our initiative—of a resolution on the non-application of force in international relations and banning for all time the use of nuclear weapons was a big event in international affairs. Following up this UN resolution, we declare the Soviet Union's readiness to come to terms and appropriately formalise reciprocal commitments with any of the nuclear powers on the non-application of force, including the banning of the use of nuclear weapons against one another.

We are realists and are well aware that influential circles in the imperialist world have not yet abandoned attempts to conduct policy "from positions of strength." The arms race which they have started, and which is a threat to peace, is still continuing. Naturally, our allies and we cannot but draw the necessary conclusions. However our peace-oriented foreign policy remains unchanged and in the present situation the potential of the peace-loving forces in their struggle against the forces of aggression and war is greater than ever. The Soviet Union will continue to work for détente and for consolidation of peace, persevering in its efforts to untie the knots of international tension, and working for stable good relations with countries with a differing social system. And if our policy evokes the appropriate response from them, then we shall say confidently that the détente will become stable, and peaceful coexistence—a universally accepted standard of inter-state relations. This means that peace on our planet will really become dependable, and the danger of a new world war could be removed. And the foreign policy of our Party, of our Soviet state, is focused on this aim.

The CPSU has always held, and now holds, that the class struggle between the two systems—the capitalist and the socialist—in the economic and political, and also, of course, the ideological domains, will continue. That is to be expected since the world outlook and the class aims of socialism and capitalism are opposite and irreconcilable. But we shall strive to shift this historically inevitable struggle onto a path free from the perils of war, of dangerous conflicts and an uncontrolled arms race. This will be a tremendous gain for world peace, for the interests of all peoples, of all states.

While expressing its constant wish to co-operate in safeguarding peace with all governments willing to do so, the Soviet Union has been steadily expanding co-operation with the peace-loving public, with the peoples of all countries. Ever new opportunities of promoting peace arise for public organisations and mass movements. And the Soviet public will continue to take an active part in their useful work. We are convinced that the forthcoming World Congress of Peace Forces will play a prominent part in the peoples' struggle for peace.

Comrades, on this glorious jubilee of our state it is with a feeling of great pride for the Soviet people, for our Leninist Party, that we read the following evaluation of the country's foreign policy, which was formulated in the early period of the existence of the USSR: "The federal state thus created on the basis of the fraternal co-operation of the peoples of the Soviet Republics sets itself the aim of preserving peace with all nations." This was said in the Address of the Presidium of the Central Executive Committee of the USSR entitled "To All the Peoples and Governments of the World", issued on the formation of the Soviet Union. It also said: "A natural ally of oppressed peoples, the Union of Soviet Socialist Republics seeks peaceful and friendly relations, and economic co-operation with all nations. The Union of Soviet Socialist Republics sets itself the aim of promoting the interests of the working people of the whole world. On the vast expanses from the Baltic, Black and White Seas to the Pacific Ocean it carries forward fraternity among peoples and affirms the rule of labour, striving at the same time to facilitate friendly co-operation among the peoples of the whole world."

Half a century has passed. The whole world has seen that they were not simply high-sounding words. The Soviet Union is faithful to the cause of socialism and peace, to which it pledged allegiance in the hour of its birth. And on the momentous day of the 50th anniversary of the Soviet Union we again declare to the whole world: The Communist Party, our state, the Soviet people shall continue to hold aloft securely the banner of its Leninist foreign policy, a policy of peace and friendship among the peoples!

## IV.

# THE SOVIET UNION FOLLOWS
# THE PATH CHARTED BY THE 24TH
# CPSU CONGRESS

Dear comrades,

For almost two years the Soviet people have been working
to carry out the decisions of the 24th Congress of the CPSU,
which charted a wide-ranging programme for our country's
economic and social progress. The tasks that were set by the
Congress are immense in scale and extremely complex. We
Communists are not ones to sit quietly. We want to do as
much as we can to improve the life of the people, for their
happiness, and to do it as quickly as possible. This is clearly
one of our Party's distinguishing characteristics.

Another is that the Party not only fights for the people's interests but is capable of rousing and carrying along the broadest masses of working people. And the people are responding
with enthusiastic activity and mass labour heroism.

During these pre-anniversary months there have been in-
numerable and diverse examples of socio-political and labour
initiatives. These wonderful initiatives have come to the
fore in various spheres of industry, construction, transport
and agriculture in all parts of the country during the emulation drive to mark the 50th anniversary of the USSR in a fitting manner. Many enterprises, towns, regions and territories
have undertaken to fulfil the annual plan ahead of schedule

by raising labour productivity, by bringing enterprises and plant units up to their rated capacities ahead of schedule and by stepping up output without increasing the number of workers. Agricultural workers have pledged to exceed the planned deliveries of grain and cotton to the state. Among the forms of labour emulation that have emerged are the "contract of thousands" movement in light industry, the emulation movement under the motto "15 Republics—15 Shock Work Shifts" and many, many others. All this, comrades, is a true fountain of popular initiative, an inexhaustible source of our society's vitality.

Communist construction produces real heroes of labour, who personify our Soviet way of life. They set magnificent examples of remarkable conscientiousness, of a communist attitude to labour. From this rostrum I would have liked to name our modest, dedicated working people who are devoting all their strength and ability to the people's cause. But this, regrettably, is physically impossible to do, comrades. Their numbers run to thousands, tens of thousands and millions. There is not a single production collective, district, area, region or territory, not a single republic that does not have foremost workers who are adding to the glory of our country by their deeds. Fine sons and daughters of our Motherland, they are marching in the front ranks of the builders of communism, and their example is followed by millions of working people. Soviet people are proud of them, applaud them and emulate them.

The Party Central Committee and local Party, government, trade union and Komsomol organisations have done much to popularise on a nationwide scale the fine initiatives displayed by the working people. For the past few months the pages of newspapers and the newscasts on TV and the radio have been reminiscent of communiques from the field of a great battle. Various contingents of working people from all parts of the country have reported on the fulfilment of their commitments and on their achievements in labour emulation.

The results of the nation-wide emulation movement in honour of the 50th anniversary of the USSR show that the working people of the Soviet Union have fulfilled their pledges, that they have come to the glorious jubilee with fine labour achievements. The successes of the winners in the movement have been acclaimed by the Motherland. Over 3,000 workers' collectives have been awarded Jubilee Badges of the Central Committee of the CPSU, the Presidium of the Supreme Soviet of the USSR, the Council of Ministers of the USSR and the All-Union Central Council of Trade Unions. Let us congratulate the recipients, comrades, and wish them further glorious achievements in the work for the welfare of the Soviet people.

We are approaching the end of the second year of the five-year plan period with results denoting a considerable growth of the key industries. Suffice it to say that in 1972 alone industrial production was double the output during all the pre-war five-year plan periods. In 1971 and 1972 our factories put out half as much again as they did in the first two years of the preceding, eighth five-year period.

Many new achievements mark the creative work of the Soviet people during these two years. Some of them may be justifiably called historic.

The 6,000,000 kw Krasnoyarsk Hydropower Station on the Yenisei, the largest in the world, is already operating at full capacity with a high degree of efficiency. This hydropower station's capacity is three times that of the largest hydropower station abroad. Meanwhile, near Moscow, on the ancient soil of Tver, the Konakovo State District Power Station has been brought to its full capacity. This 2,400,000 kw station and the over 4,000,000 kw combined capacity of the Ladyzhin State District Power Station, the Saratov Hydropower Station and the Estonian State District Power Station, which came into operation in recent years, represent a considerable contribution to the power economy of the European part of the Soviet Union.

The second section of the Volzhsky Auto Works named in honour of the 50th Anniversary of the USSR in the town of Togliatti was put into operation in January 1972. The third section has just been completed, on the eve of the anniversary. Today this modern enterprise, which employs tens of thousands of skilled workers, technicians and engineers, has a production capacity of 660,000 cars annually. This is a major achievement of our automobile industry.

The building of another giant—the heavy-duty lorry factory in the town of Naberezhniye Chelny on the Kama—is in full swing.

Our oil and gas industry has continued to grow rapidly. Soviet people are opening up vast nature's treasure-stores in Western Siberia, Kazakhstan and Uzbekistan drawing ever greater wealth from them. The increment, alone, in the oil output during the past two years has amounted to 44,500,000 tons, which is more than the Soviet Union's entire oil output in 1950. Such are our rates of growth. Such is the scale of our work.

Now, a few words about our agriculture. You are well aware, comrades, that our Party, Government and the entire Soviet people are making every effort to ensure a steady growth of agricultural output. Much was achieved in the eighth five-year plan period in keeping with the decisions of the plenary meeting of the Central Committee in March 1965 and of the last two Party congresses.

On the whole, we have been able to create incentives for agricultural workers to boost farm production and secure a definite growth of the profitability of crop and livestock farming. Collective and state farms now have greater material and technical resources and a stronger economy, and a noteworthy growth in crop yields and in the productivity of livestock farming has been achieved.

This is the economic aspect of the issue. The other and no less important aspect, the social aspect, is that during these years there has been a substantial improvement in the standard of living of the rural population, who make up a considerable proportion of the Soviet people.

The three main components of the Party's present policy in agriculture are: comprehensive mechanisation, chemisation and large-scale land improvement. For these purposes we have allocated more funds than ever before for agriculture. The targets are being successfully realised all along the line. Almost all the tractor and other farm machine factories are now being reconstructed and new and more powerful and more efficient farm machinery is being manufactured. Under the present five-year plan the country's output of mineral fertilisers is to be increased by 60 per cent. Irrigation and drainage schemes have been launched in many parts of the Soviet Union and this work is proceeding on an ever-growing scale.

As you are all aware, the weather this year was exceptionally unfavourable. The cold and snowless winter was followed by an unprecedented drought over a considerable area of the country. In the European part of the USSR there were large areas where the grain and other crops were destroyed.

In this difficult situation the Party took all the necessary steps. To the havoc wrought by the elements was opposed the conscious will of millions of Soviet people, who, organised by the Party, gave battle to nature with powerful modern machines. All forces were mobilised in order to bring in the grain harvest quickly, to avoid losses, and to ensure feed for the livestock.

A special responsibility devolved on the working people of Kazakhstan, Siberia and some regions in the Urals, where a good crop was grown. There it was important to ensure the swiftest possible harvesting because any unexpected frost or snowfall would have threatened loss of the harvest. A movement under the stirring slogan "Lose not an hour and not a gram" was launched by the agricultural workers in the Eastern regions. A real battle was begun to bring in the grain.

The working people of Siberia, the Urals and Kazakhstan did not let the country down. They fully justified its hopes and trust. They grew an excellent crop and worked selflessly to harvest it. The agricultural workers of Kazakhstan gave the country over 1,000 million poods, i.e., more than 17 million

tons of grain. The grain-growers of Siberia and the Urals delivered nearly 17 million tons of grain to the state, with the
Altai Territory alone accounting for over 5 million tons.
Thanks to good organisation and efficiency quite a good harvest was collected and the plan for the sale of grain to the
state was overfulfilled by a number of regions and Autonomous
Republics of the Centre and South of the Russian Federation,
the Ukraine, the collective and state farms of Byelorussia, Moldavia, the Baltic Republics, Transcaucasia and Central Asia.

As a result, the country's total grain harvest came to 168
million tons—over 10,300 million poods. This is somewhat
above the annual average grain crop achieved in the eighth
five-year plan period. State purchases amounted to 60 million
tons—the volume fixed in the plan, but this figure, of course, is
less than what we expected to receive under more or less
normal conditions.

We must make special mention, too, of our fine cotton-
growers. Their work this year was not at all easy. The weather
was unfavourable for cotton as well. But this did not intimi-
date the producers of white gold. At Party meetings, production conferences and at the inter-republican meeting in Tashkent the cotton-growers of Central Asia, Kazakhstan and
Azerbaijan undertook demanding commitments. They pledged
to give the people 7,135,000 tons of cotton, that is, more cotton
than last year, when there was a bumper crop. They worked
hard, with dedication. And they kept their word. They not
only fulfilled but overfulfilled their commitments. The cotton
crop was the largest in our history. A total of 7,300,000 tons
were sold to the state. Of this quantity Uzbekistan alone ac-
counted for 4,700,000 tons.

We can say with every justification, comrades, that, deeply
understanding the country's requirements, the working people
of our collective and state farms respond to the Party's call
with concrete deeds and feats of labour. These feats are highly
appreciated by the Party and the Soviet people. It is very sat-
isfying to note that a large number of foremost agricultural
workers have recently been awarded orders and medals, and

that many of them have been awarded the title of Hero of Socialist Labour. Honour and glory to these outstanding workers!

Comrades, the experience of this year, which was extremely unfavourable for agriculture, has given further convincing evidence of how our country has matured and how strong and healthy our developed socialist society has become.

In pre-revolutionary times or in the early years of Soviet power such a severe winter and such a long drought would inevitably have had the most grievous consequences, bringing disaster to many regions. Today, as life shows, we have the strength to cope with such difficulties. What formerly would have been a catastrophe is today a difficult but nonetheless surmountable obstacle in our development.

Scientists and experts have calculated that had the technology of our agriculture been at the 1955 level, under the weather conditions that were experienced this year, we would have harvested only about 90 million tons of grain from our present crop area. The fact that this year we have obtained 168 million tons is a considerable achievement in itself. It is an indication of the increased efficiency of our crop farming and of better organisation of the work of collective farmers, state-farm workers and agronomists, and is the result of the extensive assistance agriculture has received from our industry, a result of our common efforts to promote agriculture.

Of course, we have sustained certain losses on account of the failure of the grain and potato crops. But they can and must be made good by hard work in agriculture and industry. Difficulties unquestionably exist, but the normal course of the life of the country and its citizens will not be disrupted. We shall continue to take steps to maintain the necessary level of supplies to the population.

The past year, comrades, has forcefully confirmed that our Party has been correct in taking the line of consolidating the material and technical base of agriculture. Moreover, it has convincingly shown that the planned measures must be implemented at a faster rate, and that the efforts in this direction must be multiplied.

This year's experience has shown that the least losses caused by nature's whims were suffered by farms that observe all the rules of good agricultural practice, have an efficient seed-growing department, correctly apply fertilisers and use irrigation facilities. In short, where the work was well organised, the consequences of the drought were not so severe. Therefore, comrades, while Mother Nature will always be there we also have to work, and the best weapon against the vicissitudes of the weather is efficient management and active, selfless labour.

The aim set by the Party is to raise our agriculture to a level where it will fully correspond to the potentialities of modern machinery and the requirements of communist construction. We will achieve this goal by the concerted labour of our agricultural workers, by ever broader assistance to the countryside from industry, by the efforts of the entire people under the Party's leadership.

It is the dedicated labour of Soviet people in industry and agriculture and their labour achievements that make it possible to consistently carry out the programme approved by the Party Congress for raising the people's standard of living. You are well aware, comrades, of the many measures that have been taken in this direction. Let me quote only two examples: in 1971 and 1972 nearly 34 million people received increases in wages, pensions and scholarship grants. In the same two years some 23 million people received new flats.

Thus, on the whole, we are witnessing an impressive growth of the Soviet Union's economic might, and this cannot fail to gladden all of us. On this great anniversary we can and must give full voice to our achievements. But on great holidays and on routine work days we see not only our achievements but also our weak points and shortcomings, and we call these to the people's attention and direct their efforts towards removing them as quickly as possible. Regrettably, we still have shortcomings.

There is hardly any need to list them in detail today. We Communists are self-critical people and have time and again spoken seriously and specifically of these shortcomings. The main shortcoming is that to this day our vast internal reserves and intensive and qualitative factors are being inadequately and to some extent inefficiently utilised in the country's economic development. Labour outlays and also outlays of raw and other materials are being reduced only slowly in some industries, at many factories, building projects, and collective and state farms.

The central task today is to effect a radical change in orientation, to switch the accent to intensive methods of economic management and thereby substantially raise economic efficiency. The point here is that economic growth should be achieved increasingly by raising labour productivity and accelerating scientific and technological progress, by fuller utilisation of operating production capacities, by increasing the return on every ruble invested in the economy, and by more rational use of every ton of metal, fuel, cement and fertiliser.

This is the substance of the switch in economic policy as required by the 24th Congress of the Party. It is only on this foundation that the huge tasks set for the country's economic development during the current five-year period can be carried out. It is only by stepping up efficiency in the economy that adequate means and resources can be found to ensure a considerable rise in living standards and at the same time, rapid economic advance in the future and maintenance of the country's defence capability at the proper level.

The Party knew full well that the attainment of the five-year plan targets would require hard and extensive work, immense energy, a high level of organisation, a creative approach and daring in the solution of any problems that might arise. For that reason it was repeatedly stressed that if we did not raise our entire economic activity to a higher level and did not achieve a real turn towards greater economic efficiency it would be difficult to carry out the set tasks. Further, everybody knows the main directions in which we must move. These are to improve planning and the entire system of management, and to create economic conditions that will compel ministries and enterprises to adopt the maximum plan, mobilise reserves and work more efficiently. There is a wide field here to engage for our State Planning Committee, ministries and other state organisations.

The people to whom the Party has entrusted the leadership of the various sectors of our economic activity are called upon to steadily improve the methods and style of this leadership. They must, in the full sense of the word, acquire a feeling for what is new, display initiative and make use without delay of all the possibilities being opened up by scientific and technological progress. The implacable Bolshevik attitude to shortcomings and to indifference in work, and a deep sense of Party responsibility for obtaining the highest economic return with the least outlay of resources must become essential qualities of every executive.

Comrades, we are marking the anniversary of the USSR on the eve of the New Year. The coming year is of special significance. It is the third and in many ways the decisive year of the five-year plan. The task is not only to cope successfully with the basic targets of next year's plan that were endorsed a few days ago by the Supreme Soviet of the USSR, but also substantially to surpass these targets and create the necessary reserves for subsequent years.

How can this be achieved? First and foremost, by making use of the large available reserves, about which we have already spoken. This must be done by observing strict economy, by concentrating our efforts and material resources on projects nearing completion and by strengthening labour discipline and improving the organisation of work.

But this is still not all. The best plans will not be fulfilled if those who work with machine-tools or in the fields, on livestock farms, in research institutes or the service industries do not throw themselves into their work. The energy of highly organised labour multiplied by love of one's country, of the socialist Motherland, can work wonders. This is how it was in our country during the first five-year plans, the Great Patriotic War and in the years of postwar rehabilitation and peaceful construction, years marked by the mass heroism and labour enthusiasm of the people.

Today, too, a powerful tide of socialist emulation is sweeping the country. The workers of foremost collectives, livestock farms, teams and collective and state farms have pledged to increase the output and sale to the state of livestock products. In Krasnodar Territory agricultural workers have initiated a socialist emulation movement for increasing the yield of grain and other crops. Workers of leading enterprises have joined in the socialist emulation movement to achieve high indices in the work of all branches of industry, construction and transport.

In this connection I should like to draw your attention to the following. As the active creative initiative of the people, socialist emulation requires not only that foremost workers be given every support and encouragement but also that the identity of those who lag behind or work less than conscientiously be made known. This must be done publicly so that people will know not only about those who work conscientiously and energetically but also about those who work in a lackadaisical fashion, without enthusiasm. There are cases where some people talk the loudest when commitments are undertaken, but fall silent when the results of the fulfilment of these commitments are summed up, especially when these results are not very good. It so happens that everybody knows the winners, but there seem to be no losers. This kills the very idea of emulation, of actual labour competition, of actual labour rivalry, in other words, the factors to which Lenin attached special significance.

Matters must be organised in such a way as to make the drive for a high level of labour productivity, for the best indices in production and for high quality, a nation-wide cause.

We appeal to the working people of town and countryside and frankly say: the fulfilment of the 1973 plan is in your hands, comrades. We are confident that our working class, farmers and intellectuals will respond to the Party's call with further labour achievements and that they will spare no effort to secure the successful fulfilment of the assignments for the third, decisive year of the five-year plan.

Dear comrades, while concentrating attention on our immediate, current tasks, we do not lose sight of the prospects of our future progress. This the Bolsheviks have never lost sight of. In April 1918, when Soviet power had only just been established, when the fires of the Civil War were raging and everywhere there was devastation, Lenin appealed "for the speediest possible compilation of a plan for the reorganisation of industry and the economic progress of Russia." This was both natural and vital, for the October Revolution had been accomplished in order to build socialism, and socialism is inseparable from scientific economic planning.

All the more vital, then, is far-sighted scientific planning of economic and social development now that the Soviet Union is engaged in the building of communism. Under these conditions long-term planning is a matter of vital importance. As you know, this is mirrored in the decisions of the 24th Congress of the CPSU.

This year, in accordance with the Directives of the Congress, the CPSU Central Committee and the Council of Ministers of the USSR adopted a decision on the compilation of a long-term plan for the Soviet Union's economic development in 1976–1990. Work on this plan (to continue until 1975) is a major economic and political task. Lenin said in connection with the state plan for the electrification of Russia that a long-term plan of economic development is, essentially, the Party's second programme. It seems to me that this is how we must approach the issue also in this case.

Today it is difficult, of course, to be specific about the details of a long-term plan, to give precise figures. That is the aim of a painstaking scientific elaboration of the plan. Our planning bodies have a big job before them and it will be a serious test that will be judged by the Party and the country. In such a matter subjective wishes and approximations are not only valueless but even dangerous. However, the main directions, the historical contours of a long-term plan are clear. They are determined by the socio-political and economic tasks laid down in the Party Programme and in the decisions of the latest Party Congress, by the task of creating the material and technical basis of communism and substantially raising the standard of living of the Soviet people.

It is obvious that our long-term plan will, furthermore, provide for the widest utilisation of the latest achievements of science and technology in all spheres of the national economy for the benefit of the whole people and for a further very considerable rise in labour productivity, because this, as Lenin emphasised, "in the last analysis . . . is the most important, the principal thing for the victory of the new social system."

It is also obvious that thought must be given to achieving the most rational distribution of the productive forces in the country. Today, when the task of levelling up the economic development of the various republics has been in the main completed, we have the possibility of approaching economic problems principally from the standpoint of the interests of the state as a whole, from the standpoint of raising the efficiency of the entire national economy of the USSR, with due consideration, naturally, for the specific interests of the Union and Autonomous Republics.

Lastly, the long-term plan must take into account such a favourable feature of the present-day international situation as the broad development of the international division of labour and, above all, the economic integration of the socialist countries.

These are some of the considerations involved in compiling the plan for the USSR's economic development up to the year 1990. In carrying out this plan we must raise the standard of living of the Soviet people to a level that will vividly demonstrate to all, even the most diehard sceptics, the possibilities and advantages of our system in all spheres of social life. In this period the Soviet Union will without doubt make further substantial advances in science and in the field of culture, in the all-round development of the individual and in the protection of the people's health. This cannot be otherwise, for in the compilation of all our plans the guiding principle of the Party and the Soviet Government has been and continues to be: Everything in the name of man, everything for the benefit of man.

Those, comrades, are our targets. Those are the prospects before the world's first country of victorious socialism. Such is the forward march of the Union of Soviet Socialist Republics, whose 50th anniversary we are marking today.

Comrades, as progress is made in building the material and technical basis of communism and raising the people's standard of living, increasing importance attaches to the task of shaping men's consciousness, of fostering in every Soviet citizen the qualities needed in the builders of communism.

During the years of Soviet power the lives of the people have been immeasurably enriched and there has been an equally great rise in the cultural level and in the level of their political consciousness. The entire course of our history since the October Revolution has demonstrated the high moral and political qualities that have been developed in Soviet people, and the great deeds which the Soviet citizen, the free, conscientious worker, patriot and internationalist is capable of accomplishing. This is one of the most valuable achievements of socialism.

However, all this does not mean that all the political, educational and ideological tasks facing our socialist society have been carried out. It is no secret that to this day social sores, inherited from the past and essentially alien to socialism, such as an unconscientious attitude to work, slackness, indiscipline, greed and various violations of the standards of the socialist way of life not infrequently make themselves felt. The Party feels that it is its duty to draw the attention of our entire society to these things, to mobilise the people for a determined struggle against them, and to eradicate them, for unless we do this we shall not be able to build communism.

The very essence of communism lies in the high degree of

political consciousness, a sense of responsibility to society and other high moral qualities possessed by citizens. That is why the education of all citizens in a spirit of social consciousness is one of the fundamental components of the building of communism.

Today this kind of education is also imperatively demanded by economic factors. The present level of our socialist economic development and the level achieved by scientific and technological progress demand not only a high level of purely professional skill but also labour discipline, precision and organisation. Without these things we simply will not be able to cope with the extremely complex tasks posed by modern life.

Comrades, we are not building a land of idlers where rivers flow with milk and honey, but the most organised and most industrious society in human history. And the people living in that society will be highly industrious, conscientious, organised and politically conscious. We are thus faced with enormously important work and it will probably take quite a long time because human psychology is remade much more slowly than the material foundations of life.

The Party is conducting this work on an increasingly broad front and will continue to do so. In this sphere practically everything is important—the right atmosphere in family life, competent organisation of the educational process, a healthy atmosphere at the place of work, efficient everyday services, and much else. An important part is played, of course, by people working in the field of culture, in art and in the mass information media. The trade unions, the Komsomol and other mass public organisations have always been the Party's active assistants in its ideological and educational work. Today they have still more responsible tasks in this sphere.

Comrades, the great advantage possessed by Communists and generally by all politically conscious citizens of our society is that they have a sound understanding of the substance and direction of social development and clearly see the objectives that the country has set itself and the road along which we are travelling. It is a matter of honour for these advanced members of our society to share with every Soviet citizen this understanding, their ideological conviction and their fervour.

Success in the building of communism depends in many ways on the development of the Marxist-Leninist theory, which is our unerring scientific compass. The decisions of the congresses and plenary meetings of the Central Committee of our Party and major Party documents are an example of the creative development of Marxism-Leninism. But the very character of the tasks confronting us demands an increasingly active elaboration of the theoretical problems of social development and a creative approach to all aspects of life. These words of Lenin must be the motto of every Marxist: "There can be no dogmatism where the supreme and sole criterion of a doctrine is its conformity to the actual process of social and economic development."

As, in industry and agriculture not a single advance can now be made without the aid of the latest achievements of science, so, in the life of our society the development of science is the indispensable basis for the adoption of decisions and for day-to-day practice. The Party continues, as it has always done, to support the innovative, Leninist approach to the study of complex social phenomena and the efforts of our theorists to develop social theory and creatively analyse reality.

We are confronted with extensive work, comrades, in our state development and in the further promotion and improvement of socialist democracy. The basic directions of this work were outlined in the Resolution of the 24th Congress of the CPSU. This means that there must be a still more active, mass participation of the people in management, fuller implementation by the Soviets of their diverse functions in the administration of social life; a more consistent application of the principle of the accountability of executive bodies to representative bodies; further strengthening of socialist legality; an improvement in the work of the people's-control bodies.

One of the major questions of the further development of the Soviet Union that we shall have to resolve in the immediate future is that of the Constitution of the USSR.

Each of our Constitutions has been a further step forward in the development of the socialist Soviet state, a new phase in the development of socialist democracy. The 1918 Constitution of the RSFSR legislatively recorded the birth of the state of the dictatorship of the proletariat created by the October Revolution. The 1924 Constitution of the USSR was the first Constitution of the multinational Soviet state and it formalised the voluntary union of the fraternal Republics in a single state. The present, 1936 Constitution reflected the abolition of the exploiting classes and consolidated the victory of socialism in our country.

But life moves on. During the three-and-a-half decades that have passed since the adoption of that Constitution fundamental changes have taken place in the development of Soviet society, in world development and in the alignment of the class forces on the international scene. What is the main substance of these changes? Briefly speaking it consists in the following.

Instead of only the foundations of a socialist economy we now have a mature and technically well-equipped economic system in both town and countryside. This system has been developed under conditions of victorious socialism, i.e., since the adoption of the 1936 Constitution.

With the working class retaining its leading role, there has been in our country a marked convergence of all classes and social groups, and the social homogeneity of socialist society has continued to grow. The considerable distinctions between manual and non-manual work and between working and living conditions in town and countryside are being rapidly erased.

Since the war, our society has made tremendous progress in its cultural development. Today there is total literacy in the Soviet Union, with two-thirds of the working population having a secondary or a higher education.

There has been considerable headway in the promotion of

socialist democracy: law and order has been strengthened, legislation has been developed, and the role and activity of the Soviets have been enhanced.

All these fundamental changes have enabled our Party to draw the conclusion of theoretical and political importance, that a developed socialist society has been built in the Soviet Union by the dedicated labour of the Soviet people under the leadership of the Leninist Party. Having completed its great, historical mission the state of the dictatorship of the proletariat has gradually grown into a socialist state of the entire working people, with the working class remaining the leading force. The world's first country of victorious socialism has been the first to start the practical work of building communism. There have also been far-reaching changes in the Soviet Union's international position.

There are grounds for considering that all these changes in the life of our Motherland and the tasks confronting our society under the new conditions should be reflected in the Constitution of the Union of Soviet Socialist Republics. We have spoken of this before, and the appropriate preparatory work is now being done. It is the opinion of the Party Central Committee, the Presidium of the Supreme Soviet and the Council of Ministers of the USSR that it is time to complete this work. We expect to submit the appropriate proposals for the new text of the Constitution for nation-wide discussion before the next Party Congress.

This will certainly be a great, historical event in the life of the Soviet Union. It will not only help Soviet people and the world to get a better understanding of what we have achieved and sum up the results of what we have accomplished, but will also shed new light on the further progress of our Soviet socialist society advancing to communism.

*  *  *

Dear comrades, a remarkable, historic road has been traversed during the past half-century by the Union of Soviet Socialist Republics, founded by Lenin, the home of almost a quarter of a thousand million free and equal people belonging to over 100 nationalities. Soviet people have every reason to love their great Motherland and to be proud of her. This noble feeling of love for the Soviet Motherland has permeated the speeches of representatives of all the nationalities of our country at the anniversary meetings that have been held during these days throughout the Soviet Union and the hundreds of thousands of letters from the working people dedicated to the glorious anniversary.

During the imperialist world war 58 years ago Vladimir Ilyich Lenin countered the unbridled chauvinism fanned by the exploiting ruling classes with a proletarian, communist understanding of national pride. He wrote about the national pride of the Great Russians, i.e., of the Russians, who could justifiably be proud of the glorious revolutionary traditions of their people, of the deeds of heroes of the liberation struggle, of heroes who came from their midst. That is how Lenin, true son of the Russian people and a great internationalist revolutionary, understood the feeling of national pride. He called upon class-conscious Russian proletarians to be faithful "to the proletarian brotherhood of all the nations of Russia, i.e., to the cause of socialism."

Today, half a century after the formation of the Union of Soviet Socialist Republics, we can justifiably speak of a broader concept, of the great sense of patriotism of all our people, *of the national pride of the Soviet man.*

The arrogant idea of one nation being superior to another, let alone the madness of the notion of national or racial exclusiveness, is alien and odious to Soviet people. Soviet people are internationalists. That is how they have been educated by the Party and by our entire reality. But regardless of nationality or language, all Soviet people are proud of their great Motherland, which ushered in a new era in mankind's history. They are proud of the inspired labour of millions, who, under the leadership of the Communists, have built a new, truly just and free society and created a fraternal, unbreakable union of many peoples. They are proud of the exploit of the millions of heroes—sons and daughters of these peoples—who laid down their lives in the joint struggle for these gains. They are proud of the great achievements of emancipated labour, of the achievements of science and the flourishing of culture which assumes diverse national forms, of the entire way of life of the Soviet people, who have shown mankind new horizons and new moral values and ideals.

The national pride of the Soviet man is a sentiment that is great, all-embracing and immensely rich in content. It is more far-reaching and profound than the natural national feelings of each of the peoples making up our country. It has absorbed all the finest accomplishments of the labour, courage and creative genius of millions of Soviet people.

The whole country takes pride in the labour achievements of workers and collective farmers, in the outstanding discoveries of the scientists of all our Republics, in the skill of the craftsmen, in the immortal creations of the folk art of each of the fraternal nations. The fine original works of literature, painting and music of each of the peoples of the Soviet Union have long since been our common property, comrades. All this and so much more that is simply impossible to list comprises the integral and common incalculable national wealth of Soviet people. Justifiable pride is taken in all this by every Soviet citizen, by all the sons and daughters of our great multinational country, by all the peoples living in it.

The farther we advance in the building of communism and the more diverse and stronger become the economic, cultural and other ties linking all the peoples of the USSR the stronger and deeper will be the noble sentiment of the great community—the national pride of the Soviet man.

Comrades, it would be impossible to overestimate the contribution that the Union of Soviet Socialist Republics, created on Lenin's initiative, has made to the history of mankind in the course of half a century under the leadership of the Communist Party. The fact that the USSR was the first to build a socialist society and was the first to demonstrate in practice the real meaning of equal fraternal relations between peoples, will undoubtedly be remembered and valued by all peoples for all time to come.

Today the Soviet Union is forging further ahead.

The Soviet Union is moving toward communism.

We know that the road to it will not be easy. Utmost exertion of the efforts of each of the peoples of our country and of all of them together will be needed. We know that great and inspired labour, organisation and a high level of political consciousness will be required. We also know that the Soviet people possess all these qualities and will be able to display them and achieve the great goals that have been set. The guarantee of this is our common firm determination to complete the work started under Lenin's leadership in the legendary days of the October Revolution. The guarantee of this is the united will of the Soviet people, which has found its expression in the policy of our Leninist Communist Party.

# Part VIII

SPEECH AT A DINNER IN HONOR OF
COMRADE LE DUC THO ON JANUARY 30, 1973

## SPEECH BY L. I. BREZHNEV, GENERAL SECRETARY OF THE CPSU CENTRAL COMMITTEE, AT THE RECEPTION IN THE KREMLIN, ON JANUARY 30, 1973

Dear Comrade Le Duc Tho,
Dear Comrade Nguyen Duy Trinh,
Esteemed comrades and friends,

It is with profound satisfaction that our Party, the Soviet people, all our country have hailed the signing of the agreement on ending the war and restoring peace in Vietnam. This is a great victory for the Vietnamese people rallied around the Vietnamese Working People's Party, a great victory for the forces of peace, a victory of realism and common sense in international affairs.

These days the thoughts and feelings of the Soviet people are turned to the heroic Vietnamese people. We think of the Vietnamese—the men and women, the old and the young, we think of the living and the dead, of all those who upheld the righteous cause of the freedom and independence of their country in the course of the long dedicated struggle against the barbarous aggression.

These days our thoughts and feelings are turned to the fraternal socialist countries, communist and workers' parties, to the international working class, the national liberation movement, to all progressive people of the world. Their vigorous

actions against the American aggression and effective support
for the Vietnamese people brought nearer the hour of victory.

We Soviet people who went through the grim trials of the
Great Patriotic War (1941–1945), can well appreciate and
hold dear the feelings of the Vietnamese. Together with you,
dear friends, we rejoice that bombs are no longer being
dropped over your towns and villages, that for the first time
in many years the sky is clear over Vietnam!

The victory of Vietnam shows that it is impossible to con-
quer a people who fight for their freedom and independence
with the powerful support of their class brothers, of all revolutionary and progressive forces of the planet. Such a people is
invincible.

The victory of Vietnam is indicative of the tremendous vital
force of socialism. Protecting their socialist gains and upholding the right to run their own affairs, our Vietnamese brothers
displayed great dedication, staunchness and courage.

The victory of Vietnam is graphic proof of the effectiveness
of the internationalist policy of the Soviet Union and other
socialist countries. We have rendered our Vietnamese friends
active assistance in their struggle on all fronts—military, political and diplomatic.

Another important conclusion: the victory of Vietnam shows
how limited are the possibilities of imperialism in our days. By
now there are no means by which it could have reversed the
course of history!

A decisive step has been made toward the complete restoration of peace on Vietnamese soil. The Democratic Republic
of Vietnam is returning to creative work. It now is able to
focus all its efforts on building socialism, and new prospects
are opening for carrying out President Ho Chi Minh's behest
—to build a peaceful, reunited democratic Vietnam.

The way to peaceful democratic development, establishment
of genuine independence and pursuit of a policy of national
concord and unity is now opening up for South Vietnam.

More favourable conditions are appearing for stopping the
bloodshed in Laos and Cambodia.

The struggle for ending the war in Vietnam has been an extremely important issue of our foreign policy course, the Peace Programme advanced by 24th CPSU Congress. An end has now been put to the war. A very dangerous, or, to be precise, the most dangerous, hotbed of war on our planet is being eliminated.

For many years the forces of aggression and reaction have been using this war to aggravate international tension and step up the arms drive. This has greatly impeded the establishment of broad international cooperation.

New possibilities are now being afforded for promoting a détente and strengthening security and world peace. It is to be expected that the political settlement in Vietnam will exert a positive effect on relations between the states which, in one way or another, had been drawn into the events in Indochina. Moreover, this example shows that a peaceful and just solution may be found to other conflict situations, and that the still remaining hotbeds of war danger may be done away with, particularly in the Middle East where the situation is fraught with great danger to peace.

Everybody is aware of the significant improvement that has come about of late in the political climate in Europe. A beginning has been made to the changeover from tension and confrontation to business-like cooperation between states with different social systems. The policy of our country, the common policy of the fraternal socialist countries did much to make this possible.

Détente in Europe may now clearly be followed by a relaxation of tension in another vast area of the world, Asia, where the flames of war have not abated for the last few decades.

Working for a lasting peace we attach decisive significance to the further strengthening of the unity, solidarity and coordination of the actions of socialist countries. It was important yesterday, in the conditions of war in Vietnam, and it is no less important today when peace has to be stabilized and it is necessary to make the utmost progress in realizing the peoples' hopes.

Our principled line is to strengthen the unity and solidarity of socialist countries. This line has nothing in common with the policy of blocs, with building up restricted military groupings directed against the interests of other states. Our unity, as before, is wholly at the service of the cooperation of all nations, at the service of the peace and progress of mankind.

Comrades, the Paris agreement has come into force. The Central Committee of the Vietnamese Working People's Party and the DRV Government, the National Liberation Front of South Vietnam and the Provisional Revolutionary Government of the Republic of South Vietnam have declared solemnly that they will strictly abide by all its clauses. The peoples expect that the other participants in the agreement will respect and fully carry out their commitments. The forthcoming international conference, in which the Soviet Union will actively participate, will play an important role in this regard.

We know that Vietnamese workers, farmers and intellectuals will have to do a great deal to raise the cities and villages from the ruins, to rehabilitate industry and to score new successes in building socialism. Soviet people fully support the resolve expressed in the Address of the Central Committee of the Vietnamese Working People's Party and the Government of the DRV with regard to turning the Democratic Republic of Vietnam into a mighty and prosperous socialist country and still further enhancing its international role.

Dear Vietnamese comrades, in peace-time, just as in war-time, we shall stand side by side with you. Support to Vietnam is our internationalist duty. It is the common cause of all socialist countries.

Trials which no other nation has experienced since World War II fell to the lot of Vietnam. Assistance to Vietnam can and must become an act of solidarity by peoples and states regardless of their social system.

Comrades, allow me, on behalf of the Central Committee of our Party, the Presidium of the USSR Supreme Soviet and the Soviet Government and on behalf of all the Soviet people to congratulate once again our comrades-in-arms—the Vietnamese Communists, the working people of the Democratic Republic of Vietnam, and all the progressive and democratic forces of Vietnam—on their victory.

## DATE DUE

| 10/1 | | | |
|------|---|---|---|
| NOV 2 7 1978 | | | |
| | | | |
| | | | |
| | | | |
| | | | |
| | | | |
| | | | |
| | | | |
| | | | |
| | | | |
| | | | |
| | | | |
| | | | |
| | | | |
| | | | |
| | | | |
| GAYLORD | | | PRINTED IN U.S.A. |